Elisa Morgan is so refreshingly real that you immediately feel like you've found a friend who "gets" you. This is more than just a nice Christmas book. It moves past icing and sugarplums to get to the realities of why we need a Savior, and why His love is the best thing that could ever happen to us. *Christmas Changes Everything* puts forward the true heart of Christmas (and the personalities behind it) in a beautiful, biblical way. I will be reading it for Christmases to come, and giving it again and again.

—James Banks, author of *Prayers for Prodigals*

Elisa Morgan wraps her unique bundle of insights into this gift to us. She offers her rich blend of sharp biblical insights, vivid personal stories, and transformational questions I've come to expect since working with her on *Discover the Word*. All make *Christmas Changes Everything* unlike any other reflection on the arrival of Jesus Christ. Whether read to children, discussed in groups, or poured over alone, it is a gift that keeps on giving us meaning to celebrate—from the first Noel to this one!

—Rasool Berry, host of the *Where Ya From?* podcast

How can we, like the characters in the original nativity story, be changed by Christmas? With heart-warming and sometimes challenging stories, Elisa Morgan invites us to enter into the wonder of Christmas. We too can accept, yield, believe, wait, and rejoice—and be forever changed by our loving God.

—Amy Boucher Pye, author of *Celebrating Christmas*

I love this book. The portraits of each of the biblical characters in the Christmas narrative are compelling all on their own, but the real heart-stopper for me is the "Change point" at the end of each story. Elisa Morgan ushers us gently yet firmly toward cracking our hearts open to the God who desires to be born there anew. I believe these stories can change everything!

—Leslie Leyland Fields, author of *Forgiving Our Fathers and Mothers*

As Christmas rolls round each year, perhaps, like me, you wonder if there's anything new you can learn from its profound yet much-told story. Well, with this delightful book in your hands, there is more to learn. Elisa's rich exploration of each Christmas character, combined with her truly winsome storytelling, shows how Jesus's birth and childhood changed all who witnessed it—and will change us deeply too. *Christmas Changes Everything* is a breath of fresh air this yuletide season.

—Sheridan Voysey, author of *Resilient Faith* and *Resurrection Year*

christmas changes everything

HOW THE BIRTH OF JESUS BRINGS
HOPE TO THE WORLD

Elisa Morgan

Our Daily Bread
Publishing.

Library of Congress Cataloging-in-Publication Data

Names: Morgan, Elisa, 1955- author.
Title: Christmas changes everything : how the birth of Jesus brings hope to the world / Elisa Morgan.
Description: Grand Rapids : Our Daily Bread Publishing, [2022] | Includes bibliographical references. | Summary: "Elisa Morgan explores how their stories point to the change we can experience as we learn to say yes to God with confident hope and true joy"-- Provided by publisher.
Identifiers: LCCN 2022006184 | ISBN 9781640701892 (paperback)
Subjects: LCSH: Christmas. | Jesus Christ--Nativity. | Bible.
  Gospels--Biography.
Classification: LCC BV45 .M6445 2022 | DDC 242/.335--dc23/eng/20220325
LC record available at https://lccn.loc.gov/2022006184

Printed in the United States of America
23 24 25 26 27 28 29 30 / 9 8 7 6 5 4 3 2

To Evan—
After Jesus, you're my favorite Christmas gift ever!

CONTENTS

When Christmas Becomes Christmas

My eyes opened to darkness. Still! When would it *ever* be morning?

I flipped my nine-year-old self toward the wall, squeezed my eyes shut, and tried to go back to sleep. Again. Hours before, my sister and I had listened as my mother read *The Night Before Christmas* and then slipped into sugar-plum-filled dreams. Now I wrestled with impatience on this not-quite-yet Christmas morning.

Sigh. Butterflies flitted in my tummy as I imagined creeping down the hallway in our ranch-style home in Houston, Texas. I could hardly wait to see what Santa had left for us! I pictured the three red felt stockings hanging from the mantle—the names scripted in white stitching for my older sister, younger brother, and me, the middle child. They'd been flat and flimsy the night before, but now they would bulge with an orange, nuts, candies, and a few surprises. Our single-mom family opened presents on Christmas Eve, but there were always a few more Santa surprises displayed about our family room on Christmas morning. Perhaps a makeup kit for my sister. A bright red car for my little brother. And for me? Oh, how I wanted a basket of pretend but real-looking fluffy kittens!

After we discovered our treasures from Santa, we enjoyed hours of uninterrupted play. Late in the day we gathered around a table heaped with turkey, dressing, and mashed potatoes. Green and black olives would cap my fingertips until I scooped each into my mouth and made way for pumpkin pie.

I loved Christmas. Or at least, I loved what I thought was Christmas.

Cranberry bread. Tinsel covering a real evergreen tree. Our black cocker spaniel bedecked in a red velvet bow. Shiny ball ornaments displayed in a crystal bowl in the living room. Steak and baked potatoes on Christmas Eve, and turkey and trimmings on Christmas night. Sometimes my grandparents made the drive down from Fort Worth, their Oldsmobile heavy-laden with glittering gifts. My father would send a check from faraway Florida, for which my appreciation would grow as I got older. Christmas cards arrived, were opened, and then were Scotch-taped in the shape of a tree to our family room wall next to the piano. *The Andy Williams Christmas Album* blared from our stereo as we decorated the tree. *Rudolph the Red-Nosed Reindeer*, *Frosty the Snowman*, *A Charlie Brown Christmas*, and *How the Grinch Stole Christmas!* each offered thirty-minute slots of holiday entertainment on December Friday nights.

I loved it!

Yet when Christmas became Christmas, everything changed. Sure, some things stayed the same: decorations and presents and celebration and family and choirs and fun. But a deeper meaning grew in my heart and soul as I discovered that what I'd always thought of as Christmas was simply an outer wrapping containing a better gift than I'd ever imagined. I dug around in the tissue and decorative packaging of Christmas and discovered something—Someone—greater. A glorious reality that would never be put away after the holiday and its glittery celebration had passed.

For me, Christmas became Christmas in a gradual shift from year to year as I grew up. A move from the awesome moment atop Santa's lap at the department store to a growing wonder as my mother lit a candle and read a special book to us before bed. *The Little Drummer Boy. The Shiniest Star. Santa's Greatest Gift.* With the turn of each page, my mind wondered a bit more. Who was this baby Jesus? Why was He so special? What did it mean that Mary and Joseph rode on a donkey to a safe place to give Him birth? Why shepherds and wise men? Why angels and stars?

Looking back at five-year-old me and then ten-year-old and even teenage me, I know now that Christmas didn't really become Christmas to me until Easter became Easter. It took standing face to face with the stunning sacrifice of God's Son on a cross—for me and for my sin—to grasp the *real* meaning of Christmas. The anguish. The pain. The utter devastation of His heart in separation from His Father. The miraculous coming to life on Easter morning when Jesus conquered death once and for all. For all of us.

God's death and resurrection at Easter transported me back in His story to a new understanding of God's birth in a manger. Christmas became Christmas when I realized the true gift: God came as a baby who would grow up and live and die and be raised from the dead for me. I responded with a heartfelt *yes!* A yes that became an offering of my own gifts to others at Christmas out of my love for Him.

When did Christmas become Christmas for you? When did it shift into more than Santa and stockings and presents? When did it convert into more than choirs and candles and carolers? When did Christmas morph into more than family? Perhaps you're still on the edge of Christmas, wondering about its real meaning, longing for more than the window dressing offered in our world.

When Christmas becomes Christmas, it changes everything!

In the pages to follow, we'll look at the central figures portrayed in the Christmas story in Scripture and discover how Christmas became Christmas to each . . . and how that discovery changed everything in their lives. We'll explore how

- Christmas changed Mary from a virgin to the mother of our Savior who accepted God's invitation for her life.

- Christmas changed Joseph from a grieving fiancé to a committed husband and the stepfather of Jesus who yielded his way to God's.

- Christmas changed Zechariah from a man who doubted to a father who believed in God's faithfulness.

- Christmas changed Elizabeth from a disgraced, childless woman who wondered about her worth to a rejoicing mother who saw God's favor fulfilled in her life.

- Christmas changed the shepherds from lowly workers watching over lambs to men called to worship the Lamb of God and share the good news of His arrival.

- Christmas changed Simeon from a waiting man to a fulfilled follower.

- Christmas changed Anna from a woman who worshiped in fervent hope to one who worshiped with experienced conviction.

- Christmas changed the Magi from those seeking truth to those who discovered the Source of all truth.

- Christmas changed Herod from a man who could discover faith and find freedom to one who rejected learning and instead followed after fear.

When Christmas becomes Christmas, it changes you and me. From the moment we first thrill to its twinkly promise of something more than the ordinary to our discovery of the true hope of the holy night, we come to receive its real gift of sacrifice and salvation.

Christmas changes everything. It gives meaning to our meanderings, wonder to our wanderings, and joy to our journeys.

May this be a Christmas when you both explore and receive the true change—the metamorphosis—of Christmas in your heart, in your home, and in your world!

Mary's Story

Luke 1:26-55

God sent the angel Gabriel to Nazareth, a town in Galilee, to a virgin pledged to be married to a man named Joseph, a descendant of David. The virgin's name was Mary. The angel went to her and said, "Greetings, you who are highly favored! The Lord is with you."

Mary was greatly troubled at his words and wondered what kind of greeting this might be. But the angel said to her, "Do not be afraid, Mary; you have found favor with God. You will conceive and give birth to a son, and you are to call him Jesus. He will be great and will be called the Son of the Most High. The Lord God will give him the throne of his father David, and he will reign over Jacob's descendants forever; his kingdom will never end."

"How will this be," Mary asked the angel, "since I am a virgin?"

The angel answered, "The Holy Spirit will come on you, and the power of the Most High will overshadow you. So the holy one to be born will be called the Son of God. Even Elizabeth your relative is going to have a child in her old age, and she who was said to be unable to conceive is in her sixth month. For no word from God will ever fail."

"I am the Lord's servant," Mary answered. "May your word to me be fulfilled." Then the angel left her.

At that time Mary got ready and hurried to a town in the hill country of Judea, where she entered Zechariah's home and greeted Elizabeth. When Elizabeth heard Mary's greeting, the baby leaped in her womb, and Elizabeth was filled with the Holy Spirit. In a loud voice she exclaimed: "Blessed are you among women, and blessed is the child you will bear! But why am I so favored, that the mother of my Lord should come to me? As soon as the sound of your greeting reached my ears, the baby in my womb leaped for joy. Blessed is she who has believed that the Lord would fulfill his promises to her!"

And Mary said:

> *"My soul glorifies the Lord*
> *   and my spirit rejoices in God my Savior,*
> *for he has been mindful*
> *   of the humble state of his servant.*
> *From now on all generations will call me blessed,*
> *   for the Mighty One has done great things for*
> *   me—holy is his name.*
> *His mercy extends to those who fear him,*
> *   from generation to generation.*
> *He has performed mighty deeds with his arm;*
> *   he has scattered those who are proud in*
> *   their inmost thoughts.*
> *He has brought down rulers from their thrones*
> *   but has lifted up the humble.*
> *He has filled the hungry with good things*
> *   but has sent the rich away empty.*
> *He has helped his servant Israel,*
> *   remembering to be merciful*
> *to Abraham and his descendants forever,*
> *   just as he promised our ancestors."*

CHAPTER ONE

Accept

On December 21, 1978, Evan Morgan got down on one knee and proposed to me. I knew the moment was imminent as we'd made no secret just where the trajectory of our relationship was headed: marriage. But I didn't know exactly when I would become betrothed to my beloved.

We first met one fall morning in grad school, in seminary to be specific. I'd journeyed north from Houston, Texas, to Denver, Colorado, to attend Denver Seminary in response to what I sensed was God's call on my life. Evan had moved south from his native Laramie, Wyoming, after a similar nudge. We met in Old Testament class, and I have to admit that my distraction in meeting Evan left me with a permanent "brain-limp" in putting together those pieces of the Bible!

When December rolled around, we knew we'd be married. I awaited Evan's proposal with jittery expectation, so when he invited me to a special dinner at a fancy restaurant atop Flagstaff Mountain in Boulder, Colorado, I dug in my closet for a nicer-than-normal dress and added a few extra touches to my makeup. This must be it! Sure enough, in a secluded alcove in the restaurant lobby, Evan dropped to one knee, opened a ring box before my widening eyes, and asked me to be his wife. I accepted. What a Christmas gift!

In those days, weddings were modest and minus the mortgage-sized budgets. Church ceremonies spilled over into basement receptions with cake and nuts, followed by a dash for a waiting car and a quick honeymoon. Still, engagement-land spread out before us with hours of poring over *Bride* magazine, dress shopping, and showers. Engaged! I was engaged! That Christmas of my engagement changed me from unattached to attached, from single to partnered, from independent to interdependent.

For Mary, the season of engagement turned out to be even more life-defining—because into Mary's life circumstance, the very first Christmas of all time arrived. As Mary accepted God's invitation and said yes to His proposal that she would bear the Messiah, Christmas changed Mary from a betrothed virgin to the mother of our Savior. Christmas was born in her being and, through her, into all the world.

Christmas changed everything for Mary. Who was this woman? And just how, exactly, did Christmas change everything for her?

Who Was Mary?

We first meet Mary in Luke, chapters 1 and 2. Most commentators believe that Mary herself was one of Luke's primary sources for his gospel account. If that's true, then we get our understanding of Mary from her own perspective.[1]

Mary was a virgin. Luke introduces her first off with this label, *virgin*, meaning of course that she'd never had sexual relations (v. 27).

Mary was pledged to be married to a man named Joseph. In first-century Jewish culture, marriages were often arranged by families at birth or in childhood. Young girls became "betrothed" early in puberty, sometimes as young as twelve years old. Betrothal held the significance of our modern-day marriage and was only dissolvable by legal divorce. While the betrothal period lasted a year and consummation of the marriage was deferred until after the wedding, the couple was considered "husband and wife" from the moment of betrothal. Any violation of the betrothal vows had the same serious consequences as a violation of the actual wedding vows, and dissolution of this pledge was only possible through a legal divorce.[2]

Mary was young, just a girl, likely around twelve or thirteen. I know, I already said this, but it bears repeating. Can you imagine? Likely, she was from a peasant class of agricultural workers that endured the triple tax burden of Rome, the Jewish temple, and Herod.[3] Still likely living with her parents during the betrothal season, Mary was dependent on them and their provision.

Mary was highly favored by God. The angel uses this description in verse 28 and then repeats it in verse 30 as he tries to comfort the shocked young girl. To be "highly favored" is literally to have been much graced by God. What a stunning statement! And then the angel pairs the compliment with "the Lord is with you." Further comfort!

Mary was greatly troubled. The term means something like "confused, perplexed, and mentally disturbed."[4] Who wouldn't be? My friend and *Discover the Word* cohost, Bill Crowder, explains Mary's mindset: "*Perplexed* means 'deeply distressed' and *pondered* comes from the same word as our word *dialogue*. She was, in fact, reasoning with herself, in her own mind, about the meaning of all this."[5]

Mary had plenty to be distressed about and plenty to ponder. There were the obvious concerns of the biological obstacle of her being a virgin and the scandal of being an unwed mother. But Mary also would have known that pregnancy itself was a dangerous state for women in her day. Further, a large percentage of newborns didn't survive their first month, and fifty percent did not live beyond age five.[6] Such pondering, or processing, served Mary well through her life as she carefully pieced together all God was doing in and through her and all God would allow in the life of her beloved son.

Mary was informed. All Jews grew up expecting a Messiah, but no one knew where and when and from whom He would appear. The angel sent by God is identified as Gabriel (v. 26), a name given in Scripture to the angel who appeared to Daniel (twice), to Zechariah (we'll look at how Christmas changed him in an upcoming chapter), and to Mary.

Gabriel offers Mary various facts about the baby she will conceive. He will be called *Jesus*, meaning "God saves." He will be great—a reference to the status of His importance. He will be called "the Son of the Most High," which means that He will have the same qualities as Yahweh since, in Jewish thought, "son of" meant being a carbon copy of the father.[7] And He will be a descendant of David and sit on David's throne, reigning over Israel in an unending kingdom (vv. 30–33).

Mary was dumbfounded with astonishment. Mary responds with a curious and amazed wonder, "How will this be since I am a virgin?" (v. 34). Note that Mary's question is not asked in doubtful skepticism. Instead, she has an innocent curiosity about how such a thing will be accomplished, especially since she is a virgin.

Mary was obedient. As Mary struggles with the specifics of her biological questions, the angel informs her further, reiterating that God himself will father the child by "overshadowing" her. This same word is used of the disciples being covered by a cloud during the Transfiguration in Luke 9:34. Gabriel points to the unlikely pregnancy of her relative Elizabeth as proof of God's ability to accomplish the seemingly impossible. A closing statement crescendos Gabriel's explanation: "For no word from God will ever fail" (1:37).

On hearing this, Mary's obedience bursts forth in agreement, "I am the Lord's servant . . . May your word to me be fulfilled" (v. 38). The literal translation of *servant* means that Mary is saying, "I am the Lord's handmaiden, a female slave."[8]

Mary was a woman who trusted. In the moments between Gabriel's pronouncement and her agreement, Mary likely considered a huge gap of reality that would need to be bridged. How would her beloved Joseph respond to the news she was pregnant? Would he divorce her? Step away? How would her community and family receive the news and then treat her as a result? Mary had much to lose and yet she evidenced a soul sold out to the God she had come to understand through her training and upbringing: Yahweh.

From the details in her "song" of praise in verses 46–49, we can tell that she knew the Scriptures and worshiped the Lord God. Mary's song—the Magnificat—echoes Hannah's prayer of thanksgiving for Samuel (1 Samuel 2:1–10) and David's song of praise when God delivered him from Saul and other enemies (2 Samuel 22).

"My soul glorifies the Lord
and my spirit rejoices in God my Savior,
for he has been mindful
of the humble state of his servant.
From now on all generations will call me blessed,
for the Mighty One has done great things for
me—holy is his name. (Luke 1:46–49)

Mary was teachable. Luke's telling of Mary's story weaves her relationship with Elizabeth through her pregnancy (vv. 26, 39–45). God does not leave her alone but rather placed her in a mentoring relationship with an older woman who could support and guide her. And Mary received Elizabeth's blessing: "Blessed are you among women, and blessed is the child you will bear! . . . Blessed is she who has believed that the Lord would fulfill his promises to her!" (vv. 42, 45).

Mary was strong. When forced to head to Bethlehem with her husband while nine months pregnant, she makes the ninety-mile, three-day journey through a desert landscape (atop a donkey, we suppose) and then gives birth in a strange place (2:4–7). Likely these parents found shelter in the far end of a guesthouse where animals were kept close to their owners for the night.

Mary also endured Simeon's prophecy when she presented Jesus in the temple: "A sword will pierce your own soul too" (v. 35). Then, when Jesus was still under two years old, in the middle of the night, she joined Joseph in fleeing to Egypt after he was warned in a dream to escape Herod's murderous plot (Matthew 2:13–15).

Her greatest suffering, experienced face to face with her son when most other disciples had fled, would come as He was tortured and then crucified on a cross like a criminal (John 19:25).

Mary was, and still is, a woman of influence. Other than Eve, Mary is perhaps the most well-known woman who ever lived throughout the whole world. More is written about her in the Bible than any other woman. She left a powerful legacy through how she lived her life. Quietly. Daily. Mightily. Mary's influence was ever-expanding—

originating in the innermost circles of her first-century life connections and then extending globally over a multigenerational world history.

How Did Christmas Change Mary?

Mary accepted God's invitation in her life. She said yes to birthing Christmas and as a result, Christmas changed everything for her. How did Mary respond with such an astoundingly sold-out yes at such a young age?

Twice in the space of just one chapter, Luke underlines the key to Mary's acceptance. "Mary treasured up all these things and pondered them in her heart" (Luke 2:19). We see these words again when Jesus is twelve years old and Mary and Joseph take him to Jerusalem, "His mother treasured all these things in her heart" (v. 51).

To treasure means to "store up," to remember as a mother does when she writes down every detail in a baby book. To ponder, a word we described above as coming from the same word as *dialogue*, can also mean to "place together."[9] Jean Fleming suggests that the Greek means "placing together for comparison," with the word picture that Mary held all that was happening in a precious bundle, which she unpacked over and over again on the table of her heart.[10]

Ah . . . we begin to understand that Mary's yeses were not blind submission, and they certainly were not her only response. She likely said yes while also asking, *What?* And yes while simultaneously asking *Why? How?* Hers was not an easy journey. She wasn't gifted with unconditional trust or instantaneous understanding that none of the rest of us have access to. Rather, we see a layered learning. Mary's first terror-struck yielding was followed by another and another. Gradually, her yeses string together into a lifetime of agreement with the purposes of God.

Mary was a deeply committed young Jewish woman who worked at her understanding and connection to the holy. She said yes to what she understood and then she leaned into what she didn't understand, yielding to God's invitation.

Her yeses weren't easier for her than they would be for any of us. Mary's suffering was unimaginable: enduring the shame of premarital pregnancy; fleeing to Egypt to escape Herod's abominable scheme to murder all male babies under two; relinquishing her twelve-year-old son to the teachers in the temple; observing both acceptance and rejection as Jesus pronounced God's kingdom and performed miracles; and ultimately yielding her son to death on a cross for the sins of all humankind.

Responding to God with one yes at a time, Mary wove each yes into a legacy of influence that today serves as a tapestry template for all people all over the world. She was an unsuspecting servant who agreed with God's purpose in one season and watched Him provide over her lifetime all that she would need to fulfill it. She lived one yes at a time.

Christmas Changes Us When We Accept, like Mary

Hidden in the folds of Mary's story come lessons we can all receive as to how Christmas changes everything. Mary said yes—one yes at a time—to God's invitations in her life.

Acceptance of God's direction is like that—layered yeses. When I stop to consider, I see this layering in my life as well. When I was sixteen, I said yes to Jesus. At twenty-two I said yes to seminary. A year later I said yes to marriage with Evan. Another year later I said yes to teaching in a Bible college, when I had no confidence that I could speak before others. Several years later I said yes to adopting first my daughter, Eva, and then my son, Ethan. When they were toddlers, I said yes to working at MOPS International and in so doing, I said yes to leading. When it was clear to me that the time had come for the next generation of leadership at MOPS, I said yes to leaving. Next, I said yes to investing in Our Daily Bread Ministries with *Discover the Word* and *God Hears Her* and writing and filming.

Not every yes has been easy. Sometimes my yeses erupt from my heart, eagerly and enthusiastically. In other moments, I stutter my way to acceptance. I bet you can trace your finger through the yeses in your days as well. To a move? To a season of unemployment? To a marriage? To singleness? To the needs of your child or grandchild?

One Christmas morning my friend, Amanda, awoke to a throbbing headache and a throat on fire. She'd already prepared most of the Christmas meal for her in-laws and other relatives, but as the morning wore on, she knew she couldn't host the gathering. They could come to her table, but she'd have to go to bed. As happy voices wafted up to her room, her heart hurt at missing out on the celebration she'd created. She knew it was irrational, but she felt excluded and even rejected from her own dining room. Turning over to fluff her pillow and try to sleep, she sensed God's nudge. Would she accept the disappointment of what she was missing and focus on how her efforts were bringing joy to her family downstairs? Her heart still hurt, but she knew her answer would be yes.

Mary lived one yes at a time, stringing together a legacy of cooperation with God, and we can do the same. We won't always understand what each yes will bring, but we can nod and move and gradually layer our yeses, handing them to God and then watching as He weaves them into a beautiful, surrendered life.

Christmas changed Mary from a virgin to the mother of our Savior who accepted God's invitation for her life. Mary began one day as a young, engaged virgin and ended it with the Son of God in her womb. She began the day dreaming of marriage to Joseph and the children they might enjoy and ended it unsure of her husband's response to her changed status. She awoke with anticipation of a new season and went to sleep with Christmas growing in her womb. Christmas changed Mary from an inexperienced child into the mother of God.

Mary shows us how to respond when God invites us to join Him in what He is doing. When we say yes to God's call on our lives, we are changed and become part of His world-changing work.

✳ ✳ ✳

Change Point: *Where today is God inviting you into the acceptance of saying yes? How could your life and your world be changed as a result?*

Joseph's Story

Matthew 1:18-25; Luke 2:1-7; Matthew 1:25

This is how the birth of Jesus the Messiah came about: His mother Mary was pledged to be married to Joseph, but before they came together, she was found to be pregnant through the Holy Spirit. Because Joseph her husband was faithful to the law, and yet did not want to expose her to public disgrace, he had in mind to divorce her quietly.

But after he had considered this, an angel of the Lord appeared to him in a dream and said, "Joseph son of David, do not be afraid to take Mary home as your wife, because what is conceived in her is from the Holy Spirit. She will give birth to a son, and you are to give him the name Jesus, because he will save his people from their sins."

All this took place to fulfill what the Lord had said through the prophet: "The virgin will conceive and give birth to a son, and they will call him Immanuel" (which means "God with us").

When Joseph woke up, he did what the angel of the Lord had commanded him and took Mary home as his wife. But he did not consummate their marriage until she gave birth. . .

In those days Caesar Augustus issued a decree that a census should be taken of the entire Roman world. (This was the first census that took place while Quirinius was governor of Syria.) And everyone went to their own town to register.

So Joseph also went up from the town of Nazareth in Galilee to Judea, to Bethlehem the town of David, because he belonged to the house and line of David. He went there to register with Mary, who was pledged to be married to him and was expecting a child. While they were there, the time came for the baby to be born, and she gave birth to her firstborn, a son. She wrapped him in cloths and placed him in a manger, because there was no guest room available for them. . .

And [Joseph] gave him the name Jesus.

CHAPTER TWO

Yield

From the vantage point of survival, I can see now that I had swallowed a myth that needed to be exposed for me—and for others who have also fallen under its power. The myth that it's possible to create a perfect life with perfect Christmases.

When I was five years old, my father sat in a white easy chair in his home office and beckoned me to his lap. He looked into my eyes and said, "Elisa, I've decided I don't love your mother anymore. We are getting a divorce." My family fell and broke, and I decided it must have been my fault. Later, in my teen years, I tried to keep my family from breaking even more when my mother struggled with alcohol. Then, even later, when I'd come to know Jesus and was nestled in my own marriage, I determined it was my responsibility to make an unbroken family with perfect holly-decked and sugar-plummed Christmases in red, white, and green.

The problem is, I'm broken. Everybody is. Even God's family was broken. So, no matter what we do, we all end up making broken families in one way or another. And experiencing broken Christmases.

Can we move beyond the inevitable brokenness we sometimes experience at Christmas? One man in the Christmas story illustrates the power of yielding broken moments to God and experiencing the transformation only He can bring.

Who Was Joseph?

The very first Christmas was a broken Christmas. Joseph's story begins with these words: "This is how the birth of Jesus the Messiah came about: His mother Mary was pledged to be married to Joseph, but before they came together, she was found to be pregnant through the Holy Spirit" (Matthew 1:18).

Who was this man who would transform from a devastated fiancé into a committed husband and the stepfather of the Messiah?

Joseph was a young man. Likely he was around eighteen years old when we meet him in Matthew 1 and Luke 2, as that was the average age of betrothal for men.[1] Joseph's name means "May God add."[2] Such a name makes us wonder about God's plan to "add" purpose and history-changing realities through Joseph's life.

Joseph was from the Davidic line. Matthew opens his gospel with the genealogy of Jesus, tracing His heritage from Joseph back to David and beyond (Matthew 1:1–17). As the Messiah had been prophesied to come from David, this is significant for Jesus of course, but it's also meaningful for Joseph's shift from seeing his dreams as broken to grasping that God was actually fulfilling prophecy.

Joseph's belonging to the line of David is also relevant when it comes to Jesus's birth story. Caesar Augustus decreed that everyone return to their hometown to register for a census. For Joseph, being from the house of David meant traveling with a heavily pregnant Mary to Bethlehem—from the town of Nazareth in Galilee (Luke 2:1–4). Such a journey would fulfill God's prophecy that the Messiah would be born in Bethlehem (Micah 5:2).

Joseph was devastated by broken dreams. As we've already discussed, in New Testament times, betrothal was a serious pledge of marriage—without sexual relations—dissolvable only by divorce. If Mary was pregnant, Joseph's dreams of a happy and hopeful marriage with her were broken. After all, pregnancy before marriage would imply that Mary had been sexually active, and Joseph knew full well that he was not the father (Matthew 1:18). How did he cope with such shattered dreams?

Joseph was faithful. Verse 19 goes on to tell us that "because Joseph her husband was faithful to the law, and yet did not want to expose her to public disgrace, he had in mind to divorce her quietly." Some translations use the word *just*, meaning "decent," to describe Joseph's faithfulness. Other translators use the word *righteous*, meaning "in right standing with God." Ancient penalties for adultery were severe. In Egypt, the person's nose was cut off. In Persia, the nose and one ear were removed. In Israel, the law called for the adulterers to be stoned to death (Deuteronomy 22:23–24). Joseph was faithful to God's ways, which would require him to walk away from the commitment.

Joseph was thoughtful. But Joseph took time to consider the situation carefully. He allowed his thinking to mature by extended and deliberate thought—almost as if meditating on the matter (Matthew 1:20). He was a reflective, careful, and thoughtful man, and in the end, Joseph found a way to be faithful both to the law and to Mary.

Joseph was merciful. He seeks Mary's best rather than his rights. He devises a plan to divorce Mary in a private manner, in order to protect her reputation.

Joseph was informed. Similar to the manner in which Mary received information, an angel appeared to Joseph and gave him specific instructions not to be afraid but to follow through with the marriage: "Take Mary home as your wife, because what is conceived in her is from the Holy Spirit. She will give birth to a son, and you are to give him the name Jesus, because he will save his people from their sins" (vv. 20–21).

Joseph was obedient. Joseph did exactly what the angel commanded: he completed the marriage commitment and took Mary home as his wife—yet he still did not consummate the marriage until after the boy, whom he named Jesus, was born (vv. 24–25). Naming a son was the equivalent to adopting a child as one's own.[3] Joseph moved from being an unrelated man in the life of Jesus to embracing his role of stepfather out of obedience.

Joseph was courageous. After the Magi's visit (a closer look is coming up in a future chapter), an angel appeared to Joseph in another dream and instructed him to get up and take Jesus and Mary to Egypt and to stay there in order to avoid Herod's murderous scheme to kill young boys. Obediently, and with great courage, Joseph uprooted his new family to a foreign land, leaving that very night (2:13–15). Once Herod died, Joseph was again instructed by an angel in a dream to return to Israel. But when he heard that Herod's ruthless and mentally unstable son, Archelaus, was in charge, Joseph feared for his family. Another dream led Joseph to settle in Nazareth (where Antipas, a more stable son of Herod, was in leadership) rather than Bethlehem, and Joseph courageously obeyed (vv. 19–23).

Joseph was a parent. Joseph adopted Jesus as his own (1:25) and shared parenting with Mary. We see him with Mary, naming Jesus and presenting the baby for circumcision and purification in the temple (Luke 2:21–24). He and Mary marveled at what was spoken over Jesus as a baby (v. 33). Years later, when twelve-year-old Jesus remained in Jerusalem after Passover, His parents went looking for Him together. When they found Him, Mary said, "Son, why have you treated us like this? Your father and I have been anxiously searching for you" (v. 48).

How Did Christmas Change Joseph?

Joseph's world was shattered by the news that his bride was with child. He knew he was not the father and must have reeled at the discovery. But Joseph yielded his dreams to the reality of God's plan and trusted Him with an unknown future. Christmas changed Joseph from a grieving, ruined, and broken-hearted groom to the committed, trusting husband of the mother of God who then accepted her son as his own.

Joseph shows us a yielded heart that looks a lot like the heart of our God: broken and yet bent on restoration.

Christmas Can Change Us When We Yield, like Joseph

There's no such thing as a perfect family or a perfect life or a perfect Christmas. Dreams shatter. Life surprises. Instead of fighting this reality—and failing—God invites us to yield by embracing it. And to discover the beauty He brings in the broken.

What broken dreams and circumstances are you facing today? Like Joseph, could you discover beauty on the other side of brokenness as you yield your plans to God's overall purposes?

I come from a broken family. And despite my very best attempts to produce a formulaically perfect second family—the reality is that I *still* come from a broken family because everybody is broken in some way or another. We are a messy bunch. Yet I love my family more than I ever thought possible, brokenness and all. I love who they are, and I love who they have made me to be.

God doesn't sweep the broken into a dustpan and discard them. God loves the broken. God uses the broken, "tenderly assembling and reassembling fallen fragments, creating us into better versions of ourselves."4 In order to reach the broken in our world, God himself broke, sending His Son into a broken Christmas, to die a broken death on a cross for us. He brings beauty in the broken.

At sixty-four, Myra learned that her son and his wife would be divorcing. She couldn't imagine her large family enduring the fracture, much less moving beyond it. As Christmas approached, Myra prayed over who to invite to her table. Of course, her son. But her former daughter-in-law? Her son's new girlfriend? Was she to overlook the wounds and poor choices? In church one day, she bowed her head and sensed God saying, "Extend your table." Myra yielded to this unexpected nudge and invited everyone. In her heart, she resolved that those who felt comfortable to join would do so, and those who didn't would decline. As for Myra, she would yield to including whoever would accept.

Christmas changed Joseph from a grieving fiancé to the stepfather of Jesus who yielded his way to God's. When we yield to God's design for our lives, even what seems to be a disaster can be used to bring hope and healing to us and to others.

✳ ✳ ✳

Change Point: *Where is God beckoning you to yield to His ways? How could Christmas change your mind and heart as you relinquish what you believe is best to what God might be allowing in your life?*

Zechariah's Story

Luke 1:5-25, 57-80

There was a priest named Zechariah, who belonged to the priestly division of Abijah; his wife Elizabeth was also a descendant of Aaron. Both of them were righteous in the sight of God, observing all the Lord's commands and decrees blamelessly. But they were childless because Elizabeth was not able to conceive, and they were both very old.

Once when Zechariah's division was on duty and he was serving as priest before God, he was chosen by lot, according to the custom of the priesthood, to go into the temple of the Lord and burn incense. And when the time for the burning of incense came, all the assembled worshipers were praying outside.

Then an angel of the Lord appeared to him, standing at the right side of the altar of incense. When Zechariah saw him, he was startled and was gripped with fear. But the angel said to him: "Do not be afraid, Zechariah; your prayer has been heard. Your wife Elizabeth will bear you a son, and you are to call him John. He will be a joy and delight to you, and many will rejoice because of his birth, for he will be great in the sight of the Lord. He is never to take wine or other fermented drink, and he will be filled with the Holy Spirit even before he is born. He will bring back many of the people of Israel to the Lord their God. And he will go on before the Lord, in the spirit and power of Elijah, to turn the hearts of the parents to their children and the disobedient to the wisdom of the righteous—to make ready a people prepared for the Lord."

Zechariah asked the angel, "How can I be sure of this? I am an old man and my wife is well along in years."

The angel said to him, "I am Gabriel. I stand in the presence of God, and I have been sent to speak to you and to tell you this good news. And now you will be silent and not able to speak until the day this happens, because you did not believe my words, which will come true at their appointed time."

Meanwhile, the people were waiting for Zechariah and wondering why he stayed so long in the temple. When he came out, he could not speak to them. They realized he had seen a vision in the temple, for he kept making signs to them but remained unable to speak.

When his time of service was completed, he returned home. After this his wife Elizabeth became pregnant and for five months remained in seclusion. "The Lord has done this for me," she said. "In these days he has shown his favor and taken away my disgrace among the people." . . .

When it was time for Elizabeth to have her baby, she gave birth to a son. Her neighbors and relatives heard that the Lord had shown her great mercy, and they shared her joy.

On the eighth day they came to circumcise the child, and they were going to name him after his father Zechariah, but his mother spoke up and said, "No! He is to be called John."

They said to her, "There is no one among your relatives who has that name."

Then they made signs to his father, to find out what he would like to name the child. He asked for a writing tablet, and to everyone's astonishment he wrote, "His name is John." Immediately his mouth was opened and his tongue set free, and he began to speak, praising God. All the neighbors were filled with awe, and throughout the hill country of Judea people were talking about all these things. Everyone who heard this wondered about it, asking, "What then is this child going to be?" For the Lord's hand was with him.

His father Zechariah was filled with the Holy Spirit and prophesied:

"Praise be to the Lord, the God of Israel,
because he has come to his people and redeemed them.
He has raised up a horn of salvation for us
in the house of his servant David
(as he said through his holy prophets of long ago),
salvation from our enemies
and from the hand of all who hate us—
to show mercy to our ancestors
and to remember his holy covenant,
the oath he swore to our father Abraham:
to rescue us from the hand of our enemies,
and to enable us to serve him without fear
in holiness and righteousness before him all our days.

And you, my child, will be called a prophet of
the Most High;
for you will go on before the Lord to prepare
the way for him,
to give his people the knowledge of salvation
through the forgiveness of their sins,
because of the tender mercy of our God,
by which the rising sun will come to us from heaven
to shine on those living in darkness
and in the shadow of death,
to guide our feet into the path of peace."

CHAPTER THREE

Believe

When I was about sixteen, my mother decided to take our little family of four to the beach on South Padre Island, Texas, for Christmas. She rented a modest beachfront condo, and we packed up a few decorations and our stockings for Santa to fill at our vacation address. Christmas Eve we peeled boiled shrimp instead of broiling steak, and Christmas Day we sat in chaise longues on the patio facing the Gulf instead of around a tinseled tree.

It was weird.

It didn't feel like Christmas. It felt like July. We drove back to Houston, and while I was grateful for my mother's efforts (what do you do with teenagers at Christmas anyway?), I felt like I'd missed Christmas.

Have you ever missed Christmas in such an unexpected way?

Maybe there's been a year—or many—when various family members were absent from your gatherings. Or when you celebrated on a day before or after the actual holiday due to work or parenting schedules. Or when life circumstances (like a blizzard or a pandemic) forced a major change in plans. The hope of Christmas seemed to evaporate a bit in your heart.

Or maybe you've missed it at a deeper level?

Maybe, year after year, you find yourself missing out on the true hope of Christmas because in some inexplicable way, you feel that God has forgotten about you. Your prayers. Your circumstances. Your needs.

At times belief becomes overshadowed by doubt. We can "miss"

Christmas because circumstances blur our vision of its meaning and reality.

What happens when we miss Christmas? Zechariah almost did.

Who Was Zechariah?

Zechariah means "the Lord has remembered."[1] Kind of ironic for a man who felt so forgotten by God that he just about missed Christmas, right?

Zechariah was a priest. Luke tells us that Zechariah belonged to the priestly division of Abijah, one of twenty-four divisions in charge of managing temple affairs (Luke 1:5). Apart from religious pilgrimages, each division served in the temple about two weeks a year, their order decided by lot (vv. 8–9). Because there were such a large number of priests, each one would burn incense in the Holy Place most likely just once in their lifetime.[2] This was a big moment for Zechariah!

Zechariah was righteous. Zechariah took God seriously, and God viewed Zechariah as righteous. Zechariah observed "all the Lord's commands and decrees blamelessly" (v. 6). The concept here isn't that Zechariah was perfect but rather that he was faithful—an interesting description since his response to the angel will be more doubting than faithful.

Zechariah was childless. Verse 13 indicates that Zechariah had long prayed for a child. Even though it seemed to be understood that Elizabeth was "the cause" for their childlessness (v. 7), he would have carried a certain degree of disgrace. Childlessness "was not unfrequently looked on as a mark of the Divine displeasure, possibly as the punishment of some grave sin."[3] Zechariah would have no heir to carry on his priestly calling. He would have no namesake to add to a family line. He would have no inheritor to take over his property and estate. I wonder if Zechariah's childless condition also plagued his identity in some ways. Did he doubt himself and his God? After all, his very name means "the Lord remembers" and yet . . . had God forgotten him? Perhaps Zechariah's unfulfilled longing for a child shrunk his faith.

Zechariah was old. Luke tells us in verse 7 that Zechariah and Elizabeth were old—very old. Imagine what being old could have meant to Zechariah. If lots were cast for which priest would enter the temple to burn incense and Zechariah had never done so, might he have considered his chances were dwindling? Had his long wait to serve in such a spot also affected his faith?

Zechariah was scared. Luke tells us that as Zechariah was praying, an angel of the Lord appeared to him, and Zechariah "was startled and was gripped with fear" (v. 12). Who wouldn't be? To be afraid in the presence of an angel was normal. But Zechariah's fear was more intense. Translated literally, "fear fell on him."[4] Perhaps he was spooked because at that very moment he'd been praying for a son, or for the coming Messiah—topics that the angel addressed right then. Maybe, since he'd never been in the holy of holies, he wondered what other miraculous revelations might be coming next.

Zechariah doubted. The angel's proclamation that Zechariah and Elizabeth would bear a son—along with all the specifics of John's missional life—left Zechariah with his mouth hanging open in blatant disbelief. He reminds the messenger that he and his wife are old—no way could they have a baby! Further, he doubted that any son born to him would restore Israel to God (vv. 16–17). Unlike Mary's awe and confused curiosity as to how she could conceive as a virgin, Zechariah's response is one of outright disbelief. He demands a sign of proof that the angel's words are true (v. 18).[5] Wait—how could Zechariah both pray for a son and doubt that God would deliver one—at the same time? Well, we can do the same, can't we? We can pray with belief for what we know God can do *and* begin to forget God's faithfulness, doubt God's character, and slip over into disbelief. Perhaps Zechariah's response came from a defensive posture of protecting himself from further disappointed hope that God would eventually remember him and his condition. Taking it even further, maybe Zechariah's belief in God twisted into disbelief as he listened to the lies that God really wasn't caring for, providing for, and remembering him.

Zechariah faced consequences. Whatever the reason for Zechariah's disbelief, it brought consequences. The angel identified himself as one beyond questioning: "I am Gabriel. I stand in the presence of God and have been sent to speak to you and to tell you this good news" (v. 19). The name Gabriel means "hero of God" or "mighty one of God." To doubt such a messenger would be to doubt God himself.[6] One commentator suggests Gabriel's wording as, "Just as I represented God to Daniel (8:15–27; 9:20–27), so I represent him to you. Now, listen."[7]

Gabriel goes on to lay down consequences for Zechariah's not believing. He told Zechariah that he'd be unable to speak until his son was born and he was named according to God's instructions. Imagine how Zechariah must have tried to explain things to Elizabeth—and his neighbors and extended family! Perhaps he used a writing tablet in those months as he did at John's naming ceremony (v. 63). But he obviously acted, and he and Elizabeth became pregnant (vv. 23–24).

Zechariah believed. Elizabeth indeed gave birth to a son. Zechariah and Elizabeth brought the boy to the temple for circumcision and naming. When the neighbors and relatives insisted the baby be named after the father, Zechariah, as was the custom, Elizabeth objected (vv. 57–61). Zechariah set things straight, writing on a tablet that his son's name would be John. Then, Zechariah's "mouth was opened and his tongue set free, and he began to speak, praising God" (v. 64). He was filled with the Holy Spirit, and his belief was then broadcast in a song of praise to God for faithfully keeping His promises (vv. 67–79).

How Did Christmas Change Zechariah?

Christmas changed Zechariah from a man full of doubts that twisted into unbelief to a father who believed in God's faithfulness. When he pushed against the angel's decree, Zechariah pushed against his own beliefs about and commitment to his God. There were significant consequences in his life as a result.

But when Zechariah returned home to impregnate his wife, his faith was refueled. As the months ticked by and the baby grew within his aged wife, faith regrew in his own heart and replaced the unbelief.

The one whose name means "the Lord has remembered" remembered God's faithfulness, believed again, and was changed. Zechariah moved from doubt to unbelief and then back to belief. From unfaithful, Zechariah returned to faithful.

Christmas Can Change Us When We Believe, like Zechariah

One of my friends made a discovery about belief that has shaped my own faith. Having received a diagnosis of stage 4 ovarian cancer one December day, Carol began looking for handholds for her own faith in her journey toward recovery. Stage 4 of any kind of cancer is a daunting diagnosis, as such a label often includes *terminal* as well.

As Carol wrestled and journaled, she noticed a Christmas plaque with the word *believe* spelled out in clear letters. Suddenly she noticed another word sandwiched within that word. Three letters, *lie*, stared back at her, darting doubts into her heart. "There's a lie in the middle of our efforts to believe," she told me. A lie that God is not good. That God does not care. That God will not be with us. Over the next several months, Carol learned to look past the word within the word, the *lie* within *believe*, and see instead the call to believe. Fifteen years later, her commitment to believe has shaped her life. She has survived.

Belief is not a formulaic miracle cure for all that ails us. But when God comes into our lives, promising to give us life to the full, He does so in a relationship of great hope and faithfulness. When we're tempted to disbelieve His goodness, we can ask Him for help in our unbelief.

Late one Christmas Eve my grown children gathered their presents and prepared to head home. We'd celebrated together on the day before Christmas due to a swap needed with my grandson's birth father. You know, the Christmas Eve–Christmas Day rotation thing. It had been a day filled with fun and the rambunctiousness of everyone huddled in our home, and I hated to see it end. The "cherry on top," though, was that the grandboys would stay over till the next morning with their granddad and me. Yes! More fun to come.

When the doorbell rang, everyone turned to look in surprise. Who on earth? I opened the door to find my grandson's birth dad on the porch, announcing he was ready to pick him up. Huh? We made a quick excuse and said we'd be right back with him, gently closing the door and staring at each other. After consulting the parenting plan (new to us all this particular year), we discovered that indeed, one grandboy was to go with his other family beginning at 9:30 p.m. on Christmas Eve.

My heart thudded heavy. I'd so looked forward to this time! As I watched him leave, my own happiness dwindled. Oh, I was thrilled that I had my other little one to enjoy—and enjoy I would—but something about shifting my expectations made me stub my feelings and slip into sadness. Doubts swirled. Didn't God know about this situation? Why hadn't He reminded me? It took some remembering of just what I really believed about Christmas to rearrange my heart.

As the front door closed behind my grandson that Christmas Eve night, I remembered God's faithfulness to provide this child with relationships of love all around him. God also turned my gaze away from the "lie" that Christmas was "over" and toward the hope that I can hold on to every day of the year: that God sent His Son Jesus to provide never-ending life for me and for us all.

In the end, Zechariah did not miss Christmas but rather entered wholeheartedly into its reality. Zechariah remembered God. He let go of the lie that God had forgotten him and believed what the angel Gabriel told him. Christmas changed Zechariah from a man of doubt to a father filled with belief in God's faithfulness.

May Christmas change us into those who believe as well.

※ ※ ※

Change Point: *How is God inviting you to reject the lie that somehow, He has forgotten you and instead believe that the miraculous good news of Christmas is really for you as well?*

Elizabeth's Story

Luke 1:5-17, 24, 39-45, 57-58

In the time of Herod king of Judea there was a priest named Zechariah, who belonged to the priestly division of Abijah; his wife Elizabeth was also a descendant of Aaron. Both of them were righteous in the sight of God, observing all the Lord's commands and decrees blamelessly. But they were childless because Elizabeth was not able to conceive, and they were both very old.

Once when Zechariah's division was on duty and he was serving as priest before God, he was chosen by lot, according to the custom of the priesthood, to go into the temple of the Lord and burn incense. And when the time for the burning of incense came, all the assembled worshipers were praying outside.

Then an angel of the Lord appeared to him, standing at the right side of the altar of incense. When Zechariah saw him, he was startled and was gripped with fear. But the angel said to him: "Do not be afraid, Zechariah; your prayer has been heard. Your wife Elizabeth will bear you a son, and you are to call him John. He will be a joy and delight to you, and many will rejoice because of his birth, for he will be great in the sight of the Lord. He is never to take wine or other fermented drink, and he will be filled with the Holy Spirit even before he is born. He will bring back many of the people of Israel to the Lord their God. And he will go on before the Lord, in the spirit and power of Elijah, to turn the hearts of the parents to their children and the disobedient to the wisdom of the righteous—to make ready a people prepared for the Lord." . . .

After this his wife Elizabeth became pregnant and for five months remained in seclusion. "The Lord has done this for me," she said. "In these days he has shown his favor and taken away my disgrace among the people." . . .

Mary got ready and hurried to a town in the hill country of Judea, where she entered Zechariah's home and greeted Elizabeth. When Elizabeth heard Mary's greeting, the baby leaped in her womb, and Elizabeth was filled with the Holy Spirit. In a loud voice she exclaimed: "Blessed are you among women, and blessed is the child you will bear! But why am I so favored, that the mother of my Lord should come to me? As soon as the sound of your greeting reached my ears, the baby in my womb leaped for joy. Blessed is she who has believed that the Lord would fulfill his promises to her!" . . .

When it was time for Elizabeth to have her baby, she gave birth to a son. Her neighbors and relatives heard that the Lord had shown her great mercy, and they shared her joy.

CHAPTER FOUR

Rejoice

One year, just a few days before Christmas, my phone rang with some news that took the air out of my holiday. The only other couple in our adoption group that hadn't yet been placed with a baby—besides us—was calling to say they had a baby. I hung up, feeling like I'd been kicked in the chest. No baby for us. Still. We'd been waiting for almost five years.

Since Evan was a cancer survivor, we'd known early on that we'd be unable to bear children. That we would become parents through adoption was a reality we'd both accepted at a very deep level. At first the wait wasn't so bad. My husband and I were busy in our careers. We loved our marriage and our lives felt *full*. But as the years passed and friends and family members entered parenthood, I began to discover an ache—a pull—a yawning hole. I wanted to be a mother.

I decided that nearly five years was a long-enough wait. Just after Thanksgiving that year, I rolled up my spiritual sleeves and begged God, "Please, God, a baby by Christmas." After all God himself *became* a baby on the first Christmas. Surely, He'd want me to have a baby by Christmas! I set up a Christmas tree in our family room, wrapped it in white twinkly lights and decorated the branches with pink and blue ribbons. I stood back to take in my work and christened it the "Hope for a Baby Tree." Every day I knelt there, pouring my plea out to God.

And then my phone rang and I heard the hard truth that no, we were not going to have a baby by Christmas. Devastated, I paused by the tree that had become a symbol of God's provision. Was God still faithful? Was I doing something wrong?

I left the tree standing well beyond Christmas and continued my morning prayer until—in late February—after some questioning from a neighbor, I took it down. On a late spring weekend, we received our baby girl. At last. I rejoiced! Our second child came some two years later in a blistering July summer. I rejoiced again!

That final childless Christmas helped me understand that while we are waiting, God is working. It may not look like it. It may not feel like it. It may not seem like it in any way we can tangibly touch. But when I look back at that devastating call on that December day, I realize that my daughter was growing in her birth mother's womb. God was indeed answering my prayer. He was working while I was waiting.

Most of us have trouble rejoicing while we're waiting. Instead, we lament. We ache and wail and cry out for help, Hannah-like. But when our eyes are opened to the gifts our good God gives—sometimes exactly the ones we were waiting for and in other moments surprising answers we didn't even know we needed—joy bubbles up and over in our hearts.

One woman in the Christmas story models for all of us a powerful posture of receiving whatever God brings us and however He brings it with rejoicing.

Who Was Elizabeth?

Surprisingly, Luke begins his gospel not with the conception of Jesus in Mary but with the conception of John in Elizabeth. In New Testament times, women were valued mainly for their ability to produce children. In short, if they were barren, they were rejected by society and considered a disgrace. How seemingly ironic, then, that Elizabeth's name means "God is my oath, or oath of God,"[1] conveying the message that "you can count on God no matter what." Who was Elizabeth?

Elizabeth was from the priestly line of Aaron. Luke underlines her identity early in his gospel (1:5). She was also related to Mary (v. 36) and lived in the hill country of Judea (v. 39).

Elizabeth was righteous in the sight of God. Verse 6 tells us that along with her husband, Zechariah, she observed "all the Lord's commands and decrees blamelessly."

Elizabeth was not able to conceive. Luke includes the reality of her barrenness, identifying her alone as the one responsible for the childlessness of her marriage to Zechariah. "They were childless because Elizabeth was not able to conceive" (v. 7). Such a state was a "disgrace" to a woman in that culture.

Elizabeth was an old woman, married to an old man. One of the most sobering descriptions of Elizabeth and Zechariah comes in verse 7 where Luke ends his opening description of the couple with the phrase, "and they were both very old." Notice he doesn't say they were elderly or up there in years—perhaps nicer expressions of their season. Nope, he says it bluntly: they were very old. And when Zechariah doubts the angel's pronouncement of pregnancy, he describes Elizabeth as "well along in years" (v. 18).

Elizabeth rejoiced in God's faithfulness. Zechariah returned home from his interaction in the temple, and Elizabeth became pregnant. She remained in seclusion for five months (v. 24), perhaps in meditative celebration of God's faithfulness, as her joyous "song to God" included these words, "The Lord has done this for me. . . . In these days he has shown his favor and taken away my disgrace among the people" (v. 25).

Elizabeth was Mary's mentor. As a relative of Mary, Elizabeth received Mary's pregnant presence into her home, welcoming her need for companionship in her plight. For three months, at least, Mary learned from this woman, old enough to be her grandmother. Elizabeth's song of praise became a model for Mary, honoring her: "Blessed are you among women, and blessed is the child you will bear! . . . Blessed is she who has believed that the Lord would fulfill his promises to her!" (vv. 42, 45). Elizabeth's joy in the face of impossibility must have strengthened Mary in her own "disgraced" state.

Elizabeth was obedient. When the crowd planned to name her baby after Zechariah, his father, as was the custom, Elizabeth spoke up, "No! He is to be called John" (v. 60). Still mute, Zechariah motioned for a writing tablet and wrote, "His name is John," and— *boom!*—suddenly he could speak (vv. 63–64).

Edith Deen, author of the classic *All of the Women of the Bible*, wrote, "What a joyful moment for Elizabeth. Her husband could speak again and at her side was a promising son. The hand of the Lord was with her."[2]

Elizabeth rejoiced in God's revelation of a child given to her and Zechariah. Unlike Zechariah in his response of disbelief, Elizabeth apparently received the news of her pregnancy in faith. She waited well, even before actually experiencing the reality of John's birth, and moved into joy based on God's promise to her and her husband.

How Did Christmas Change Elizabeth?

Elizabeth trusted God's revelation and rejoiced in the news that she would become pregnant and give birth to a son. Christmas changed Elizabeth from a childless woman who was disgraced in her society to a mother rejoicing at God's favor. She lived out the very meaning of her name, "the oath of God" by believing in God's faithfulness and rejoicing in the delight of being pregnant with God's promised baby. Blessing and joy thread throughout Elizabeth's story as "the baby leaped in her womb, and Elizabeth was filled with the Holy Spirit" (v. 41). In verse 44, Elizabeth herself shares that the baby in her womb actually "leaped for joy." In the fifth or sixth month of a first pregnancy, moms will feel the baby's movement. Elizabeth joyed at the reality of life within her and new life to come for all humankind.

God had invited her to move from a role of disgrace and rejection into favor and inclusion. And because He had, Elizabeth rejoiced. A once "empty" woman was flooded with the Holy Spirit in praise to God.

In a pinnacle of rejoicing, Elizabeth's joy then contagiously overflowed to others around her. Mary exclaimed, "My soul glorifies the

Lord and my spirit rejoices in God my Savior" (vv. 46–47). When Elizabeth gave birth, "Her neighbors and relatives heard that the Lord had shown her great mercy, and they shared her joy" (v. 58).

Christmas Can Change Us
When We Rejoice, like Elizabeth

Every Christmas since my last childless one, I've continued to set up a "Hope for a Baby Tree," tied with pink and blue ribbons. In the early years, my husband and I did the work while telling our children the tale of our waiting and wanting them so much. My children are now in their thirties, but each year I set up a miniature version of the tree, reminding myself and others to hope in God's faithfulness. I remember what God has provided, and I continue to hold on to joy.

It's not always easy to rejoice when we look at the life circumstances around us, is it? There are still so many unanswered prayers. Needs that go unmet. Painful realities. These can steal God's gift of joy to us in disappointment and pain. But I've learned that when we trust that God is actually working while we're waiting, joy becomes a byproduct. God's joy becomes His surprising gift to us. It bubbles up in us and then through us, catching others in its wake.

Except for a very brief five-year relationship, my friend Stan has spent nearly every Christmas of his adult life on his own. Since his extended family lived far across the country, for most of his single years, Stan volunteered to work the holiday shift so others could be with their families. But Stan still celebrated his faith in Jesus. On Christmas Eve or Christmas Day, at some point, he prepared a special dinner for one, poured himself a glass of bubbly, put on his favorite carols, and settled in to open the few sweetly decorated gifts that had arrived for him. He cuddled up with his faithful golden retriever, and together they watched *It's a Wonderful Life* and realized that indeed, they were having a *wonderful* life! Rather than giving in to grief over what he didn't have, Stan rejoiced in what was real all around and within him.

Elizabeth rejoiced in response to the news her husband received that she would become pregnant. At last! A disgraced, childless woman was changed by Christmas into a rejoicing mother. And as Elizabeth was changed, she allowed the joy of Christmas to flow through her out to others, changing them as well.

✳ ✳ ✳

Change Point: *Where is God wanting to produce joy in your life this Christmas? How might you both discover and experience joy right now by noticing the stunning gifts God has provided in your life, even if you are still lacking some of the elements you so desire?*

The Shepherds' Story

Luke 2:8-20

There were shepherds living out in the fields nearby, keeping watch over their flocks at night. An angel of the Lord appeared to them, and the glory of the Lord shone around them, and they were terrified. But the angel said to them, "Do not be afraid. I bring you good news that will cause great joy for all the people. Today in the town of David a Savior has been born to you; he is the Messiah, the Lord. This will be a sign to you: You will find a baby wrapped in cloths and lying in a manger."

Suddenly a great company of the heavenly host appeared with the angel, praising God and saying,

> *"Glory to God in the highest heaven,*
> *and on earth peace to those on whom his favor*
> *rests."*

When the angels had left them and gone into heaven, the shepherds said to one another, "Let's go to Bethlehem and see this thing that has happened, which the Lord has told us about."

So they hurried off and found Mary and Joseph, and the baby, who was lying in the manger. When they had seen him, they spread the word concerning what had been told them about this child, and all who heard it were amazed at what the shepherds said to them. But Mary treasured up all these things and pondered them in her heart. The shepherds returned, glorifying and praising God for all the things they had heard and seen, which were just as they had been told.

CHAPTER FIVE

Share

Every Christmas Eve, our family lights a candle atop a birthday cake (usually chocolate), inscribed with a cursive "Happy Birthday, Jesus!" and then we sing it out together. We've practiced this tradition since our own kids were toddlers, and today we continue it with our grand-kids. Sometimes others are gathered with us: a girlfriend, a neighbor, my brother, other children from other families. In the glow of candle-light, faces open to the wonder of celebration in a pedestaled cake trimmed in red and green icing.

To some, the practice might seem fluffy or even irreverent. But over the years, I've found that sharing Christmas as "Jesus's birthday" can help others understand and embrace the real meaning of this holy day. We can relate to birthdays! Presents and balloons and cake and babies connect with our everyday. Imagining Christmas as baby Jesus with a birthday brings Him close.

I so long for friends and family to come to know the very good news of Jesus. How He brings hope into dark moments and is present with us no matter what we face. How His death on the cross frees us from the worst in ourselves. While surprising to some, I've found that serving up cake with candles and singing provides yet another way I can share why Jesus is so special to me.

The message of Christmas is for sharing. Long ago, the first people who shared the news of Jesus's birthday were a group of unexpected folks.

Who Were the Shepherds?

The Bible is full of shepherds. Before he became king, David was a shepherd. Many Old Testament heroes, including Abraham, Isaac, and Jacob, were shepherds. Even some women, such as Rachel in Genesis 29:9, are described as shepherdesses. Scripture uses the image of shepherd to express how God himself cares for us, such as in John 10:14–15 where Jesus says, "I am the good shepherd . . . and I lay down my life for the sheep."

We know about these particular shepherds' experience of the first Christmas only from Luke's gospel. For some reason, Matthew omits their presence. Interestingly, we'll see in a future chapter that Matthew includes the presence of the Magi, where Luke does not. Different perspectives telling the same story!

Who were these shepherds?

The shepherds were lowly workers. Bill Crowder describes the shepherds of the Christmas story as "simple men with simple lives."[1] In Old Testament times shepherding carried some undertones of disrespect as shepherds were considered the lowest societal class (the Talmud prohibited shepherds from testifying in courtrooms).[2] By New Testament times the trade was viewed as a decent profession, but working in the field with "dirty" sheep, delivering newborns, and handling their messes meant the shepherds were ceremonially unclean and therefore cut off from society in significant ways.

This group of shepherds, stationed near Jerusalem, were likely tasked with raising lambs that were free of blemish to be sacrificed in the temple. Again, what an irony!

The shepherds were vigilant. Luke 2:8 tells us, "There were shepherds living out in the fields nearby, keeping watch over their flocks at night." The work of shepherds was to care for sheep, protecting them from invaders—both human and wild—providing food and water, and ensuring they kept themselves out of danger. Sheep are notoriously not-so-smart. Without constant supervision, they can run themselves into wily situations. Thus, shepherds lived with their flocks, taking turns to keep watch over them 24-7.

The shepherds saw an angel. As we have seen, angels are central to all aspects of the Christmas story. An angel appeared to Mary (Luke 1:26–27). In several dreams, an angel appeared to Joseph (Matthew 1:20; 2:13, 19). In his story of the shepherds, Luke writes, "An angel of the Lord appeared to them, and the glory of the Lord shone around them" (Luke 2:9). Angels are representatives of God, expressing His presence, and as such, they brought with them God's glory, or the manifestation of His power.[3] Thus, when the shepherds saw the angel appearing, they knew they were about to receive a stunning revelation of God's presence for God's purpose.

The shepherds were terrified. When the angel appeared and the glory of God shone around them, "they were terrified" (v. 9). The word here means they were in "a state of severe distress, aroused by intense concern for impending pain, danger, evil, etc."[4] In short, they were paralyzed with fear. How else would they respond? Remember they were lowly workers, raising lambs for the temple sacrifice but not personally involved in temple visitation. When the very presence of God appears to them—and they being "unclean"—of course they were terrified!

The shepherds were comforted. God does not leave them in their fear. Just as with Mary and Joseph and Zechariah, comfort comes. The angel says, "I bring you good news that will cause great joy for all the people. Today in the town of David a Savior has been born to you; he is the Messiah, the Lord" (vv. 10–11).

The shepherds were informed. Note the sign the angel gives: "You will find a baby wrapped in cloths and lying in a manger" (v. 12). Such specific details distinguished Jesus from other baby boys born at the same time.

The shepherds were mentored. A great company of angels appeared, raised their own praises, and mentored the shepherds in how to celebrate God's great provision of rescue. "Glory to God in the highest heaven, and on earth peace to those on whom his favor rests" (v. 14). That's how to celebrate: give glory to God!

The shepherds hurried off and found. Their response? No more fear! Now the shepherds exclaimed, "Let's go to Bethlehem and see this thing that has happened, which the Lord has told us about" (v. 15). They spring into action. First, Luke tells us that they hurried. I love this detail! Whether they were excited or eager or just ready to be away from the presence of the scary host, the shepherds hurried off. The idea here is that they wasted no time. Then Luke stresses that they found the baby. The verb *found* in verse 16 means "found after a search."[5] Can you picture these shepherds hiking up their robes and running from house to house in search of the baby the angels had described?

The shepherds shared. After hearing, searching, and finding, they see Jesus and they "spread the word concerning what had been told them about this child" (v. 17). As a result, "all who heard it were amazed at what the shepherds said to them" (v. 18). These lowly shepherds became the first evangelists. Luke ends his account of the shepherds with verse 20, "The shepherds returned, glorying and praising God for all the things they had heard and seen, which were just as they had been told." While they "returned," presumably to the same field with the same flocks, surely shepherding would never be the same for these shepherds.

How Did Christmas Change the Shepherds?

Christmas changed the shepherds from workers in a field to witnesses of God's plan for rescue in the Messiah of the world. They went from watching lambs that might be sacrificed for atonement to worshiping the Lamb of God who would take away the sins of the world. Then they shared the good news they'd experienced with anyone who would listen.

This first revelation of the Messiah came to a group of lowly shepherds. God's selection of these shepherds as His first evangelists mirrors

His heart of love for all, grace for all, forgiveness for all, and inclusion for all in His kingdom purposes. Into a culture that expected a Messiah to execute a kingly leadership of a royal revolution, God sent His Son as a baby to a humble couple in a quiet town, visited first by a band of servant shepherds who wouldn't even be fit to enter the temple grounds.

Christmas Can Change Us
When We Share, like the Shepherds

How can we follow after the shepherds' example and share what we've seen in Jesus? I think about this so often, especially at Christmas.

For every December of his growing up years, my husband Evan entertained strangers at the family Christmas Day dinner. His father was the dean of engineering at the local university and took great interest in and compassion on the various international students who were orphaned on the holiday. So he invited them over and for the entire afternoon and evening, the Morgan boys ate and played games with and otherwise entertained young men and women who had nowhere else to go. There were seasons when Evan admits resenting his parents' hospitality. But overshadowing any negative feelings is his understanding now that God has always intended that all His children be included in the celebration of His birth.

These days, we head to church on Christmas Eve, sometimes just my husband and me and in other years with a gang of family of varying degrees of faith. I'm always touched by the final moments of the service, the same year after year. Our pastor bends a candle toward the Christ candle in the Advent wreath on the platform, holds it up in front of his face toward the ceiling and then invites us all to participate in lighting our own candles around the sanctuary.

I bend my unlit candle to the lit one of my husband's and then turn to the person at my side, offering my light for their candle. One by one the lights catch, flicker, and glow as we sing "Silent Night, Holy Night" and the room fills with a radiance that lights the faces around me.

Year after year I'm stunned that God invites us to participate in the miracle of sharing our faith with each other and with our world. He could wave His hand and—*poof!*—catch the world on fire with His Being. But no, God bends to each heart and whispers, "a Savior has been born to *you*; He is the Messiah, the Lord." To you. And to me. And to us all.

Like the shepherds, we are to hurry and find and see . . . and then share what we have discovered. The hope of Christmas that is Jesus.

As I light the candle atop Jesus's birthday cake this year, once again, I pray that God will catch the hearts of all around me on fire with the love He died to provide.

✳ ✳ ✳

Change Point: *Is there someone special in your life whom you long to know the Jesus you know? How might you share your faith in Jesus right now?*

Simeon's Story

Luke 2:22-35

*When the time came for the purification rites required by the
Law of Moses, Joseph and Mary took him to Jerusalem to
present him to the Lord (as it is written in the Law of the Lord,
"Every firstborn male is to be consecrated to the Lord"), and to
offer a sacrifice in keeping with what is said in the Law of the
Lord: "a pair of doves or two young pigeons."*

*Now there was a man in Jerusalem called Simeon, who was
righteous and devout. He was waiting for the consolation of
Israel, and the Holy Spirit was on him. It had been revealed to
him by the Holy Spirit that he would not die before he had seen
the Lord's Messiah. Moved by the Spirit, he went into the temple
courts. When the parents brought in the child Jesus to do for him
what the custom of the Law required, Simeon took him in his
arms and praised God, saying:*

> *"Sovereign Lord, as you have promised,*
> *you may now dismiss your servant in peace.*
> *For my eyes have seen your salvation,*

which you have prepared in the sight of all nations:
a light for revelation to the Gentiles,
and the glory of your people Israel."

The child's father and mother marveled at what was said about him. Then Simeon blessed them and said to Mary, his mother: "This child is destined to cause the falling and rising of many in Israel, and to be a sign that will be spoken against, so that the thoughts of many hearts will be revealed. And a sword will pierce your own soul too."

CHAPTER SIX

Wait

My mother called on Christmas Day to say Merry Christmas. Since marrying into Evan's family, we'd begun a practice of rotating celebrations between extended family: in Houston with my mother and brother one year, and then in Wyoming with Evan's family the next. When we became parents, the grandparents began to travel to us in alternate years. You know the drill.

The Christmas she called was actually a just-our-family Christmas. Evan's parents were in Arkansas with his brother and his family. And Mother had decided not to travel to us. She'd been undergoing cancer treatment for several months and thought a quiet Christmas alone was best.

I put the phone on speaker to include Evan and the kids, and we began with the customary thanksgiving for the various gifts we'd exchanged. I'd sent her a fluffy orange bathrobe, one of her favorite at-home outfits. She loved the salmon color, which made me happy. We took turns thanking her for the gifts she'd sent. An outfit each for our daughter and son. A silver bell to add to the bell collection that she'd begun for me after our wedding. A gift card and some golf balls for Evan. Then the family members pulled away from the speakerphone, leaving just me with my mother. There was a pause, and a surprising revelation: the cancer had spread to her back. It was in her bones. She said she would have only months—which actually turned out to be only weeks—to live.

I was in my early thirties and had begun the soul-work of understanding my family of origin and grappling with what responsibilities and choices were mine to carry and which were not. Since my own embrace of God's love for me in my teen years, what mattered to me most of all was that my mother come to understand God's unconditional love for her. Hearing that she was nearing death deepened my concern. I'd been waiting sooooo long for God to nudge her heart and for her to yield and let Him love her.

Waiting seasons are stretching seasons, aren't they? We wait to get our driver's license, find a career, maybe settle down in marriage, maybe have kids, receive answers to prayers, and see loved ones come to know God. In the wait-and-see game that is life, it's tough to be content with where we are. We seem to always want what isn't yet, what we're waiting for. And few of us wait well.

The theme of waiting threads through so many of the characters in the story of Christmas. As we've seen, Elizabeth's rejoicing was birthed out of her long wait for a child. Another character in the Christmas story seemed to understand the key to waiting well. Simeon waited contentedly with hope for the heart of Christmas: the coming of the Savior.

Who Was Simeon?

Forty days into Jesus's young life, Luke introduces us to Simeon. "When the time came for the purification rites required by the Law of Moses, Joseph and Mary took him to Jerusalem to present him to the Lord" (Luke 2:22). According to Leviticus 12:1–8, Jewish law specified that after the birth of a male child, the mother was "unclean" for seven days and should seclude at home for a further thirty-three. A purification sacrifice was then offered on the fortieth day with an offering of a pair of doves or two young pigeons.

Onto this backdrop, Simeon appears in Luke 2:25. What do we know about him?

Simeon was righteous and devout. Isn't it interesting how very many of the characters we're considering fit this description? Mary, Joseph, Elizabeth, Zechariah, and now Simeon. Simeon was righteous, meaning in right standing with God. He was devout, meaning honoring God with reverence.

Simeon was waiting. Verse 25 goes on to tell us that Simeon was, "waiting for the consolation of Israel," which means "deliverance."[1] Simeon was intent on the provision of God's Messiah to bring Israel to himself. His days were filled with hopeful anticipation. He lived and breathed for this restoration of God's people. And he waited well. How did Simeon wait well?

Simeon had the Holy Spirit on him. Perhaps because God's Spirit was with him (v. 25), Simeon seemed to wait with contentment and peace. While the Holy Spirit wasn't formally "given" until Pentecost, we see His work throughout Scripture. Simeon's waiting was not the impatient wrestling of someone wringing their hands but rather a waiting that flowed from a fervent faith that God would accomplish what He promised.

Simeon received a revelation. Luke underlines that the revelation that Simeon received was from the Holy Spirit (v. 26). He gives us the impression that Simeon was old, as Simeon is told that he would not die before seeing the consolation of Israel. With a name that appropriately means "he who hears" in Hebrew,[2] Simeon spent his days and nights in the temple with a specific purpose. His hope was more than wishing and wanting. Simeon was convinced that God would accomplish what had been revealed to him: he would see the Messiah before he died!

Simeon was moved by the Spirit to go into the temple courts. In his third mention of the Holy Spirit in just a few verses, Luke tells us that God's Spirit moved Simeon into just the right place at just the right time in verse 27. Simeon went into the temple courts at a moment when he would encounter the new parents, Mary and Joseph, entering with baby Jesus to offer their sacrifice. A divine appointment for sure!

Simeon took Jesus in his arms and praised God. As Simeon reached for the baby Jesus and took him in his arms, a sense of fulfillment welled up in his heart. God had followed through on His revelation! Simeon's wait was complete! His heart was at peace. "Sovereign Lord, as you have promised, you may now dismiss your servant in peace. For my eyes have seen your salvation, which you have prepared in the sight of all nations: a light for revelation to the Gentiles, and the glory of your people Israel" (vv. 29–32).

Simeon blessed Mary and Joseph and the baby. Verse 33 uses the word *marveled*, which means to be amazed or wonder,[3] to describe the response of Jesus's parents. While they'd each received an angelic visit proclaiming Jesus to be the Messiah and they'd witnessed the shepherds' worship, this might have been the first moment when such a revelation was expressed in public. Simeon's words embraced the reality that Jesus's ministry would be to the whole world, to Israel of course but also to the Gentiles. Surely this scared them, but it must have strengthened them as well.

Simeon prophesied. Simeon's final words give us chills. Spoken specifically to Mary, who would one day stand at the foot of the cross as her son was crucified, he said, "This child is destined to cause the falling and rising of many in Israel, and to be a sign that will be spoken against, so that the thoughts of many hearts will be revealed. And a sword will pierce your own soul too" (vv. 34–35). Simeon's statement underlines the reality that what we long for can fulfill us, but it can also bring an allotted amount of suffering.

How Did Christmas Change Simeon?

Simeon's assignment was to wait, and he waited well. Christmas changed Simeon from a waiting man of hope who had been given a promise to a fulfilled person contented to die with no further items on his life's "bucket list." Because he waited with anticipation, Simeon did not miss God's provision but rather received it boldly and thanked God enthusiastically.

We're wise to take note that Simeon's passion for the deliverance of Israel was not just for himself but rather for the whole planet. Dr. Mark Young, president of Denver Seminary, expressed Simeon's experience this way, "When Simeon held that baby, he recognized that God had stepped into history in a way that God had never done before. I liken this to D-day. This was the day when God's forces, when God's work to defeat Satan began in a way that had never been experienced before."[4]

Advanced in his years and faithful to his trustful waiting, Simeon received God's promise and then gave Him glory.

Christmas Can Change Us When We Wait, like Simeon

Several weeks after that Christmas phone call, I flew to my mother's bedside in a Texas hospital room, joining my brother and sister. We sat with her for a few days as she relinquished her hold on her life here. At one point, I noticed she seemed to be looking off at an angle rather than directly at my sister who sat near her head. I assumed it was just my perspective from the other side of the room.

But when it was my turn to sit by her head, I could see that my mother was looking off to my right, not at my face. I scooted my face to my right so that she could take me in better. She reached out and gently moved me back in place. So I repeated my gesture, and she responded by repeating hers.

"Mother, do you see something here?" I asked, pointing to the empty space next to me.

"Yes, Elisa," she responded, "I see Jesus."

I'd waited all my life for my mother to "see Jesus." Here on her deathbed, she at last embraced the love God had for her.

Admittedly, I wasn't great at waiting in that season. And in the seasons since, I still have so much to learn.

In a more recent Christmas gathering, several families joined us for a "red and green" dinner (where all the food served is red and green) and a nativity acted out by our young grandchildren. My grandson, Marcus, then eight years old, was the oldest, so we knew our plan to corral the kids into a "play" was ambitious.

One of the moms took charge of the toddler sheep. Another selected the five- and six-year-olds to be Joseph and Mary. Baby Jesus was played by a Cabbage Patch doll. Marcus's job was to hold the flashlight, fulfilling the role of the Christmas star.

We parents and grandparents took our places in the family room and waited for the process to begin at the "stable" by our fireplace hearth. And wait we did. For the sheep. For the cow. For the shepherds and angels, dawdling up the basement steps and tripping over their sheet costumes. Finally, the holy couple arrived, with Jesus dangling by an arm from Mary's clenched fist. All while Marcus's arm was stretched far above his head, the Christmas star lighting the way. Massaging the ache in his arm with his free hand, Marcus muttered, "This is painful."

Yes, waiting is painful. At times it hurts, doesn't it? Simeon waited with righteous and devout faithfulness, receptive to the word of the Holy Spirit and anticipating God's fulfillment with hope. Paul writes in Romans 8:24–25, "Hope that is seen is no hope at all. Who hopes for what they already have? But if we hope for what we do not yet have, we wait for it patiently." And then when we receive that hope, we are fulfilled.

Christmas changed Simeon from a waiting man to a fulfilled follower. As we open our eyes to God's provision in our days and commit ourselves to waiting well for Him to act, may Christmas change us as well.

✳ ✳ ✳

Change Point: *Where is God asking you to wait on Him? How does the fulfillment of God's promise to Simeon help you in your waiting?*

Anna's Story

Luke 2:36-38

There was also a prophet, Anna, the daughter of Penuel, of the tribe of Asher. She was very old; she had lived with her husband seven years after her marriage, and then was a widow until she was eighty-four. She never left the temple but worshiped night and day, fasting and praying. Coming up to them at that very moment, she gave thanks to God and spoke about the child to all who were looking forward to the redemption of Jerusalem.

CHAPTER SEVEN

Worship

My son and I were sitting in church one Saturday evening in December. My husband was traveling for work, and ten-year-old Ethan was usually in children's church, but tonight he'd asked to come into the sanctuary with me. I let my eyes roam over the Advent wreath with its candles, the poinsettias outlining the dais steps, the lit Christmas trees, and the always-present roughly hewn cross. We rose to our feet, clapping along as the worship choruses began. Then we took our turn passing the offering container and settled into the sermon.

Finishing his sermon with a prayer, Pastor Robert then laid his Bible on a small table before him and picked up the pottery-formed chalice and a hunk of bread. He raised them up in a gesture of love to God and repeated Jesus's words from the upper room the night before He went to the cross for us. "Take it; this is my body. . . . This is my blood of the covenant which is poured out for many" (Mark 14:22, 24).

My wide-eyed son turned to me and asked if he could go forward for communion. Images from the past videoed through my mind. Ethan with a cotton ball-covered hat that morphed him into a lamb for the toddler's Christmas pageant. His five-year-old proclamation one day as he stood atop our fireplace hearth, "Jesus Christ is the Son of God who died on the cross for our sins!"—like a small version of Pastor Robert. His zeal for God when he returned from camp just the previous summer. Communion? I bent my mouth to his ear and asked if he understood what it meant, and he nodded. "It's what Jesus said to do." Yes, it seemed right.

The lights in the room dimmed as we took our places in the line moving toward the table that held the wafers and juice. Edging forward, I whispered to Ethan to follow my lead. He nodded in response. When we returned to our row and sat down in our pew, Ethan leaned into me with an awe-struck whisper, "That was dramatic!"

Dramatic? That word—and Ethan's experience—took me aback. He'd watched all that was going on around him and had entered into the Lord's Supper with a sincerity and a presence that left him wondrous. If I was honest, such an experience of dramatic worship was rare for me. More often, my worship of God included mouthing choruses, turning pages in my Bible to follow along with my pastor, and obediently partaking of communion. Don't get me wrong, I love God with all my heart! But truly experiencing the drama of worship, as Ethan had, was not the norm of my day, if you know what I mean.

I wondered . . . was I doing something wrong in my daily routine with God so that dramatic experiences of worship were rare? Or are the two, daily and dramatic, actually both supposed to be elements of our experience of worship?

A woman named Anna made worship her daily occupation, persevering with a focus on faithfulness. As we look at her life, we'll find that her faithfulness in the daily readied her to experience the rare drama of the unusual.

Who Was Anna?

After concluding the story of the well-waiting Simeon, in his next breath Luke introduces us to Anna. The Greek version of the Hebrew "Hannah," her name means "grace."

Anna was a prophet. It's easy to slide by this fact as we read along. There aren't many women prophets mentioned in the Bible. The Old Testament names seven: Sarah, Miriam, Deborah, Hannah, Abigail,

Huldah, and Esther. The New Testament mentions only Anna and the "four unmarried daughters" of Philip in Acts 21:8–9.

Let's pause and take this in. In Luke 2:36, Anna is described as a prophet—the daughter of Penuel (whose name means "face of God"), of the tribe of Asher, one of the ten tribes of northern Israel. In Hebrew, the word *prophet* comes from terms that together mean "seer." In general, a prophet is then one who sees and is a spokesperson for God regarding what is seen.[1] After the four hundred "years of silence," when there had been no prophetic utterance since the prophet Malachi, Anna was a woman who watched for the Messiah, ready to speak of His appearance when she saw Him.

Anna was very old. To be exact, Luke tells us that Anna was eighty-four years old (vv. 36–37). While in the Old Testament we see individuals living long lives of even hundreds of years, by New Testament times, eighty-four was a very long life. In the ancient world, old age was often associated with wisdom.[2]

Anna was a widow. In fact, Anna had been a widow for nearly all her life. How lonely she must have been! How disappointing her future must have seemed!

Our understanding of betrothal and marriage from Mary's story reveals that young girls married around puberty, age twelve to thirteen. In verses 36–37, Luke tells us that Anna had only lived with her husband for seven years, which indicates that she was around twenty when he died. We meet her when she's eighty-four. That's more than sixty years as a widow! (Some scholars translate the verses to mean that she lived eighty-four years as a widow which would make her more than one hundred years old.)[3]

Widows were not in a good position in New Testament culture. The responsibility to provide for them would fall to their children or other extended family. When there were no children or family members, as seems to have been the case with Anna, widows could become vulnerable to exploitation and neglect.

Anna invested her whole life in watchful worship. And here lies Anna's secret to experiencing a deep connection with her God: Anna was faithful to persevere in serving God in worship at the temple 24-7. Luke tells us that "She never left the temple but worshiped night and day, fasting and praying" (v. 37). The word *worshiped* here contains the concepts of religious rituals and veneration of God. It has also been suggested that she performed some work in or about the sacred building, such as trimming the lamps, which would have been regarded as a high honor.[4]

Anna's worship included the rituals of fasting and praying, but what is noteworthy is the ongoing nature of her expression to God. Luke gives us the impression that Anna was never not worshiping. She worshiped in the morning and evening, when she ate and when she rested, when she undertook daily chores, and when she carefully fulfilled religious requirements. All with the prophet's watchful vigil of observing what God was doing in and around her, making sure she wouldn't miss Him in her days. In order to devote herself so constantly, likely Anna moved from the tribe of her extended family of Asher into a room in the temple area. She made her home in the presence of God where she prayed and fasted around the clock. One scholar expressed it this way, "She made the temple her permanent home; worship, prayer, and fasting, her occupation."[5]

Anna was in the right place at the right time. Because she invested her whole life in the watchkeeping that was worship, Anna was right where she needed to be when Jesus arrived at the temple with Mary and Joseph. I love what Bill Crowder writes of her devotion. "Imagine what would have happened had she decided, 'I'm tired. I've been doing this for years. I think I'll take the day off and stay home.' But she didn't!"[6] Anna's routine practice of worship positioned her perfectly to receive the stunning arrival of the Messiah in the moment.

Anna praised. With her whole being poised in service to God, Anna did not miss the arrival of Christmas in Mary and Joseph with baby Jesus. Once she saw the holy family, she nearly exploded with joyful thanksgiving.

Luke describes Anna's seeing and proclaiming in verse 38, "Coming up to them at that very moment, she gave thanks to God and spoke about the child to all who were looking forward to the redemption of Jerusalem." While we don't know the specific words she used, Luke makes clear the content of her message. She thanked God! She shared her joy about just who this child was with all who were also looking forward to the redemption of Jerusalem. As Edith Deen put it, "This aged woman had seen God more than events, and God in events. She had seen because she was intimate with grace, providence, and redemption."[7]

How Did Christmas Change Anna?

Anna was a woman who had been alone nearly all her life. No doubt disappointed and faced with the reality of possible despair, Anna instead invested her entire life in a faithful kind of worship that involved watching for God to work. Every day. All day. Every night. All night. She turned her eyes to seeing God constantly, actually moving in to live in His presence and offering Him her complete attention. With her eyes open to His coming, however and whenever that might be, Anna saw what she was hoping for and directed the gaze of others to see Him as well.

Christmas changed Anna from a woman who worshiped in fervent hope to one who worshiped with experienced conviction. Anna turned her daily routine into a practice of ongoing worship, and her ongoing worship into her daily routine. She was present and aware when the dramatic occurred.

Because Anna watched, she saw. Because Anna saw, she shared the coming of the Messiah with others who also needed His hope. What difference could Anna's life of worship make to you and me?

Christmas Can Change Us
When We Worship, like Anna

Ethan's pronouncement of the drama of worship has lingered with me over the years. While dramatic worship remains more the exception than the norm, I've discovered that when I tune my heart into the reality of God's presence in my daily routine, I become more open to both noticing and appreciating His dramatic revelations as well. When I am faithful to God, I experience His faithfulness to reveal himself to me.

In Psalm 84, we see an illustration of how we can build our worship into our daily routine, by following after the example of nesting birds. "Even the sparrow has found a home, and the swallow a nest for herself, where she may have her young—a place near your altar" (v. 3). Maybe time with God comes when we build our home—our nest—near His altar and then live there in His presence. Pray when washing dishes. Leave a Bible open on the counter and pause to read a verse when passing by. Listen to an uplifting podcast when driving.

If we build a nest near God's altar and live there all the time, we won't have to move somewhere to be in His presence. And if we're worshiping day in and day out, as Anna did, we'll be right where we need to be to take in God's "dramatic" when it appears.

Brother Lawrence was a Carmelite monk who lived in the 1600s and published a collection of poems, essays, and prayers to help his friends learn what he'd learned: "the practice of the presence of God." We can draw close to God when we turn ordinary life activities into daily conversations with Him.[8]

When Christmas becomes Christmas, we build a faithful life of worship where we live minute to minute in God's presence. While padding across worn carpet in the morning. Cupping a mug of coffee. Breathing in the scent of soap from the shower. Laying out place settings for dinner. Looking into the face of a child or a spouse or a friend and seeing love reflected there. Driving the carpool. Completing a project at work.

Like Anna, could we turn our daily routine into worship, and our worship into daily routine? Then, when God reveals himself in a dramatic moment, we are where we need to be to see what He has to reveal to us. When we are faithful to worship God in the daily and the dramatic, our relationship with Him deepens.

✳ ✳ ✳

Change Point: *What does your worship look like? How might Christmas change your worship into an ongoing experience with God so that you are present to receive Him when He reveals himself in the dramatic or the daily?*

The Magi's Story

Matthew 2:1-12

After Jesus was born in Bethlehem in Judea, during the time of King Herod, Magi from the east came to Jerusalem and asked, "Where is the one who has been born king of the Jews? We saw his star when it rose and have come to worship him."

When King Herod heard this he was disturbed, and all Jerusalem with him. When he had called together all the people's chief priests and teachers of the law, he asked them where the Messiah was to be born. "In Bethlehem in Judea," they replied, "for this is what the prophet has written:

"'But you, Bethlehem, in the land of Judah,
are by no means least among the rulers of Judah;
for out of you will come a ruler
who will shepherd my people Israel.'"

Then Herod called the Magi secretly and found out from them the exact time the star had appeared. He sent them to Bethlehem and said, "Go and search carefully for the child. As soon as you find him, report to me, so that I too may go and worship him."

After they had heard the king, they went on their way, and the star they had seen when it rose went ahead of them until it stopped over the place where the child was. When they saw the star, they were overjoyed. On coming to the house, they saw the child with his mother Mary, and they bowed down and worshiped him. Then they opened their treasures and presented him with gifts of gold, frankincense and myrrh. And having been warned in a dream not to go back to Herod, they returned to their country by another route.

CHAPTER EIGHT

Seek

With a giddy grin across his face, Evan handed me a simply wrapped but enormous gift. Immediately I knew something was up. I'd hinted unashamedly that I'd *love* some diamond earrings for Christmas. Not the carat-sized Elizabeth Taylor version that some women were wearing. No, I'd be happy with miniscule chips set on gold posts that wouldn't irritate my ears. Just something romantic yet suitable for everyday wear. And affordable on his early ministry salary.

So, when he handed me the bigger-than-a-pair-of-earrings box that Christmas Eve at my mother's home in Houston, my heart sank a bit. But that grin . . . what was he up to? Of course, I didn't let on that I suspected something. Everyone was watching: my younger brother, older sister and her husband, and my mother. This was our first married Christmas, and I was determined to be the model of the perfect wife in our single-mom, divorced home. I pasted a smile across my disappointment and carefully unwrapped Evan's gift. Inside I found not a present at all but rather the first of what would turn out to be many clues that would take me from the living room to the kitchen to the bedroom to the bathroom, outside to our rental car, and then finally back in the house.

I followed the clues with mounting curiosity, my hopes rising with each directive that would bring me closer to that longed-for treasure.

The last clue came wrapped inside a box the size of a book, still not the right size for earrings. But its words gripped me and guided me to the kitchen. "Go to the place where you'd expect to find 'ice.'" Sure enough, tucked inside our old frost-encrusted freezer, an earring-sized box awaited my discovery. Ice for sure!

I've kept those tiny diamond studs for all of our forty-plus years of marriage. They remind me of Evan's love, his sense of humor, and his creativity. And of the pay-off that can come from fervently seeking something I truly desire.

The Magi were men who were seeking something far more precious than jewels. Their quest was for truth and as a result of seeking it, they discovered its Source.

Who Were the Magi?

The word *Magi* is a transliteration of the Greek word, *magoi*, which is best translated "wise men."[1] But the phrase *wise men* is not what we'd understand today as *sages*. Rather, the Magi were students of the stars, skilled in the "interpretation of dreams and various other secret arts."[2] We might understand them as astrologers today.

The Magi's visit was some time after Jesus's birth. Notice that Matthew refers to Jesus as a child, not an infant or baby, and that the Magi discover Him with his parents in a house, rather than in temporary housing with livestock (Matthew 2:11). Further, when we dig into the timeline of Herod's reign and his concern about a baby born as king (which we will explore in the next chapter), we know that Jesus was likely around one year old when the Magi journeyed.

The Magi came from the East to Jerusalem. Matthew reports, "After Jesus was born in Bethlehem in Judea, during the time of King Herod, Magi from the east came to Jerusalem" (v. 1). Likely this geographical reference means that these Gentile men came from a home in Arabia or Persia, perhaps in the royal courts of those lands. We think of them as a threesome after the mention of three specific gifts given to Christ, but Matthew doesn't actually mention the number in the group. In any case, historians suggest they were colorfully dressed, exotic aliens.[3]

The Magi searched for one born king. We're given the purpose of their journey through the question they pose in verse 2. "Where is the one who has been born king of the Jews?" Commentators note "the words they use mean 'born king,' not 'born to be king,' as is often said; they are talking about what he is, not what he will be."[4] The Magi were seekers of the royal. Perhaps they'd been instructed by Jewish scholars who migrated to their region with copies of Old Testament manuscripts and therefore had a special curiosity in a baby born king.[5] Clearly, they went to Jerusalem, seeking information about the specific location of the child.

The Magi wanted to worship the child. With a careful reading of this passage, we discover a dual layer within their singular purpose. "We saw his star when it rose and have come to worship him" (v. 2). In those days, a king's birth was believed to be accompanied by the presence of a celestial light over a land. No doubt, as studiers of the skies, these men were more interested in new light sightings than most.

But the wise men sought the child king not just because He was identified by an intriguing celestial wonder; they wanted to worship Him. Here *worship* means they wanted to express their allegiance to this deity.[6] These men were summoned forward to find the promised One, to meet the hoped-for Messiah, and to offer the commitment of their lives.

The Magi faced Herod. Matthew describes Herod's summoning of the Magi in verses 7–8. "Then Herod called the Magi secretly and found out from them the exact time the star had appeared. He sent them to Bethlehem and said, 'Go and search carefully for the child. As soon as you find him, report to me, so that I too may go and worship him.'"

Imagine the wise men's response. Herod also wanted to worship the child king? Could he really be acknowledging that this child's kingship was greater than his own? Did Herod's instruction further fuel their journey, or did they see his pretense for what it was?

The Magi followed a star and found the child. Tension builds as the presence of the star becomes more and more supernatural. "They went on their way, and the star they had seen when it rose went ahead of them until it stopped over the place where the child was. When they saw the star, they were overjoyed" (vv. 9–10). Imagine their reaction when they at last discovered Jesus—after such a long journey! One commentator suggests, "'Deliriously happy' may be an overstatement, but it was something like that."[7]

"Stars" (i.e., planets) naturally travel from east to west across the heavens, not from north to south, the direction the Magi traveled from Jerusalem to Bethlehem. Could it be that "the star" the Magi saw that led them to a specific house was the Shekinah glory of God? That same glory had led the children of Israel through the wilderness for forty years as a pillar of fire and cloud. Perhaps this was what they saw in the East, and for want of a better term, they called it a "star."[8]

On December 21, 2020, the "great conjunction" of Jupiter and Saturn, accompanied by a rare meteor shower, resurfaced long-held science about the possibility that the star followed by the Magi was actually a similar alignment of planets that created a "Christmas star."[9]

Whether the star's presence was natural or supernatural, it led the wise men about five miles south from Jerusalem to Bethlehem until it stopped over "X marks the spot." "On coming to the house, they saw the child with his mother Mary" (v. 11).

The Magi worshiped the child and presented Him with gifts. "They bowed down and worshiped him" (v. 11). To worship is to encounter the living and holy God and to acknowledge Him as such. It's striking that so many Jews, who awaited the coming of the Messiah, would miss identifying Him, while these Gentile seekers would not only discover His whereabouts but bow to honor His deity.

Verse 11 goes on, "Then they opened their treasures and presented him with gifts of gold, frankincense and myrrh." The meaning of *treasures* here is actually more of a treasure box—a kind of safe used to transport valuables. The Magi pull out and present gifts of gold (for wealth), frankincense (an aromatic resin), and myrrh (a fragrant spice). In some traditions, these gifts have been ascribed symbolic meanings. Gold for Jesus's divinity. Frankincense to represent the fragrance of

His life. Myrrh to represent His sacrificial death on the cross, as bodies were often embalmed with such a spice. All were "treasures" fit for a king. I wonder if these very gifts were used by Joseph and Mary to sustain their family after fleeing Herod and while in hiding in Egypt.

The Magi returned to their country by another route. After meeting Jesus in person, worshiping Him in their posture and with their gifts, and after being "warned in a dream not to go back to Herod, they returned to their country by another route" (v. 12). Here, the word *warned* is referring to a divine utterance, a revelation.[10]

You have to wonder just how many "routes" there were between Bethlehem and the home of the Magi. In any case, the reality is that after their encounter with the Christ child, they knew they had found the truth they sought and they obeyed the message of their divine dream.

How Did Christmas Change the Magi?

Christmas changed the Magi from those searching for truth to ones who were committed to the Source of all truth. Where once they'd studied the stars in their roles as astronomers, after meeting the Light of the World, they bowed, worshiped, and became students of His ways. And in knowing the Source of truth, their behavior changed. Instead of bowing to serve the evil desires of Herod's heart—the earthly "king"—they aligned themselves and their actions to the One born king. They went home another way.

Christmas Can Change Us When We Seek, like the Magi

I'm struck by how often the term *Magi* is rendered *wise men*, as if these foreigners were skilled in offering sage advice on how to live life well. The reality is that for most of their lives, these men from the East employed a skill that would be from the "dark side," as Star Wars fans might put it. They studied what was evident in their world without considering the Maker of the world.

Like many true students of life, at some point, the Magi began a pursuit of something more. What could lie behind the wonders of the world? What could explain the unexplainable?

In 1 Corinthians 2, the apostle Paul compares the wisdom of humans to God's wisdom. He differentiates the wisdom that comes from God and what we can understand on our own. "We declare God's wisdom, a mystery that has been hidden and that God destined for our glory before time began. None of the rulers of this age understood it, for if they had, they would not have crucified the Lord of glory" (vv. 7–8).

The Magi found Jesus because they sought truth. Because they sought truth, they discovered its Source. Because they discovered the Source of truth, the way they lived their lives changed. Truth changes us.

One of my relatives doesn't believe in Jesus. Well, he believes that Jesus was a real man—as far as history can prove His existence. But he doesn't believe in God. Or his need for God. It doesn't make logical sense to him. When we touch on the subject, which we do every now and then because I love this relative and I love Jesus and I want him to know that Jesus loves him, he says, "If you can prove to me that God exists, I'll believe."

You probably have someone similar in your life. A parent. A child. A friend or neighbor. What I've discovered though is that I can't *prove* God to anyone. Oh, I've tried, believe me! The issue of belief is a personal matter. And a person has to open their eyes to see the proof of God's existence around them.

But what I can do is what the Magi did. I can seek truth. I can hunt for God's ways as I would pursue a desired gift at Christmas. The writer of Proverbs says, "If you accept my words and store up my commands within you, turning your ear to wisdom and applying your heart to understanding—indeed, if you call out for insight and cry aloud for understanding, and if you look for it as for silver and search for it as for hidden treasure, then you will understand the fear of the LORD and find the knowledge of God. For the LORD gives wisdom; from his mouth come knowledge and understanding" (Proverbs 2:1–6).

Christmas changed the Magi from those seeking truth to those discovering its Source. As I hunt for truth and discover God's glorious presence all around me, perhaps others will grow curious about the Source of my peace. As I follow after the clues God leaves in my days, maybe others will notice and begin to read the clues He's leaving for them as well. As I unwrap God's gifts and respond to His leading by adjusting the direction of my life, others just may take notice and begin to wonder what they, too, might find in following Him.

※ ※ ※

Change Point: *What are you seeking this Christmas? Are you seeking it, hunting for it, as you would valuable treasure? When you back away and look at this sought-after element, is it worth the effort? Is there a way God is leaving you clues to direct you to himself?*

Herod's Story

Matthew 2:13-23

*An angel of the Lord appeared to Joseph in a dream. "Get up,"
he said, "take the child and his mother and escape to Egypt. Stay
there until I tell you, for Herod is going to search for the child to
kill him."*

*So he got up, took the child and his mother during the night
and left for Egypt, where he stayed until the death of Herod.
And so was fulfilled what the Lord had said through the prophet:
"Out of Egypt I called my son."*

*When Herod realized that he had been outwitted by the
Magi, he was furious, and he gave orders to kill all the boys in
Bethlehem and its vicinity who were two years old and under, in
accordance with the time he had learned from the Magi. Then
what was said through the prophet Jeremiah was fulfilled:*

> *"A voice is heard in Ramah,*
> *weeping and great mourning,*
> *Rachel weeping for her children*
> *and refusing to be comforted,*
> *because they are no more."*

After Herod died, an angel of the Lord appeared in a dream to Joseph in Egypt and said, "Get up, take the child and his mother and go to the land of Israel, for those who were trying to take the child's life are dead."

So he got up, took the child and his mother and went to the land of Israel. But when he heard that Archelaus was reigning in Judea in place of his father Herod, he was afraid to go there. Having been warned in a dream, he withdrew to the district of Galilee, and he went and lived in a town called Nazareth. So was fulfilled what was said through the prophets, that he would be called a Nazarene.

CHAPTER NINE

Learn

Christmas morning began at my daughter's house, and earlier than most other mornings! The grandkids were sequestered upstairs until my husband and I arrived, and then my son and daughter-in-law. We would serve as the audience to their Santa surprises. An hour or so later, we gathered for breakfast around a beautiful table covered with a black-and-red gingham cloth and tabletop trees. Our places were marked with labeled coffee mugs: Mom, Dad, Dog-lover, Coffee-drinker, etc.

Around midday, we grandparents took the grandkids to our house, and then the rest of the adults joined us for appetizers and the unwrapping blowout of family gifts around our tree. The afternoon passed with naps, a Christmas movie, me in the kitchen prepping dinner, and gift assembly in the basement family room.

We sat down to Christmas dinner just as the sun dipped behind the clouds and our candlelit table flickered in a festive glow. It had been a perfect Christmas—even though it was really Christmas Eve and we were just pretending it was Christmas Day.

Like many families, ours is a family of holiday rotations. In order to keep things simple for our grandkids, we often pretend certain days are holidays because they are the days that work for us all to gather. This was a year when Christmas Eve had become Christmas Day for us Morgans. I loved every minute. But in my heart,

I knew that it wasn't the *real* day, and in a moment of overflow, I said so to my daughter-in-law.

"This has been great!" I murmured to her as we all finished our yummy dinner. "But I can't wait till next year when we get to celebrate Christmas on Christmas!"

Tears welled in her eyes. She'd worked so hard to create a sweet celebration—we all had. But my comment somehow communicated to her that her efforts weren't enough. My words burst the joy from the day, leaving it deflated like a popped balloon. Uh-oh. I longed to scoop those syllables back up and shove them down my throat. Obviously, I'd wounded her. And diminished our celebration of Christmas as less than real in the process.

We got through the evening. The next day, the *real* Christmas Day, Evan and I celebrated alone and enjoyed the surprising blessing of a quiet and restful holy day. But my heart was heavy from the hurt I'd heaped on my dear one. God nudged me toward a realization that I wasn't wanting to embrace. *Elisa, you've had decades to be in charge of Christmas. Maybe it's time to release the traditions to the next generation . . . ?*

I didn't want to hear this. I didn't want to let go of doing Christmas the way I wanted to do it. As I've shared, Christmas was one of the things my mother did "right" in my opinion. Our traditions wrapped me in safety and happiness when the rest of the year was just plain messy. Re-enacting Christmas *my* way brought me joy.

But was it bringing others joy—the way I was intending? And by the way, did it bring joy to my Jesus, the One I hoped to celebrate and invite others to know?

It was a long day and evening of tug-of-warring with God. I sensed He wanted me to let go. I didn't want to. But I wanted to try. Late in the evening I sent out some texts, asking for forgiveness for my insistence on my own way. I offered to release our traditions to my son and daughter-in-law and to my daughter and son-in-law.

I learned a lot that Christmas. About how I sometimes don't like the lessons of Christmas—but they are always for my good. What happens if I don't learn? Or to be more specific, if I turn away and reject what God reveals?

One man in the Christmas story illustrates all too well what can happen when we reject God's advent in our lives.

Who Was Herod?

Herod was king of the Jews. Wait—what? Wasn't Jesus King of the Jews? And David and Solomon and, and, and . . . ? Let's put it this way: Herod proclaimed himself king of the Jews.

Herod was king. The Herod in the Christmas story of Matthew 2 is one of four Herods who reigned in biblical times. He was the Roman-appointed king of Judea at the time of Jesus's birth, ruling from 37 BC to AD 4. Due to his massive building projects, which included rebuilding the temple in Jerusalem and his own lavish and massive palace in Caesarea, making it the Roman headquarters in Palestine, he became known as "Herod the Great." As the first major leader of Jerusalem after its subjugation by Rome, Herod imposed heavy taxes and conscripted labor for his projects.

Herod was disturbed. Verse 3 packs a wallop. When Herod heard that the Magi were looking for the one born king of the Jews, "he was disturbed, and all Jerusalem with him." *Disturbed* is quite a descriptor! Such a word can mean more than worried—it can also imply emotional or psychological problems. Digging deeper into his background, we discover many reasons for Herod's instability. Herod was actually an Idumean (Edomite), from the line of Esau rather than from the line of Jacob, the rightful lineage. While he professed that he'd converted to Judaism, he wasn't qualified to be king by birth. As a strong military leader, a shrewd politician, and a ruthless tyrant, he rose to power by gaining Roman favor and then kept this power by suppressing through cruelty any who opposed him.[1]

His evil ways affected his own immediate family. He killed his wife Mariamme and two of his sons for what he perceived as threats on his kingdom. Caesar Augustus once said that he'd rather be Herod's swine than his son, evidently a play on words since the two words sound similar in Greek.[2] The ancient historian, Josephus, suggested Herod was both physically and mentally degenerated. His detailed writings about Herod's madness offer "the picture of an arteriosclerotic who had once been athletic and vigorous but who became increasingly prone to delusions of persecution and uncontrollable outbursts of violence, the results of hypertension and a diseased brain."[3]

Herod was disturbed in many ways, and as a result, all Jerusalem was disturbed with him. Some because they had benefited from his reign and were concerned about losing their spot in the power queue. But many other Jews were deeply concerned because while Herod professed his allegiance to God, his behavior belied his words. They knew his lineage was false, his leadership tyrannical, and his heart corrupt. The suggestion of another king—a child king—coming into power was disturbing indeed. Would Herod become even more unhinged if his power was challenged? And how would that alter their way of life?

Herod went into defense mode. Threatened by the advent of the true king of the Jews, Herod constructed a plot to stay in power. In his scheme, he made some key moves to protect his throne and yet each failed him. First, after calling together the chief priests and teachers of the law, "he asked them where the Messiah was to be born" (v. 4). Such a question revealed his ignorance of Scripture. One who had truly converted to Judaism would have known the prophecy they cited from Micah: "But you, Bethlehem, in the land of Judah, are by no means least among the rulers of Judah; for out of you will come a ruler who will shepherd my people Israel" (Matthew 2:6).

Second, Herod secretly met with the Magi to find out the exact time the star had appeared (v. 7) and instructed them to go to Bethlehem to search for the child and then report his whereabouts so that "I too may go and worship him" (v. 8). As the Magi demonstrated in their behavior, to worship means to literally bow down. But as would soon become apparent, Herod had no such desire. He was just trying to smoke Jesus out. His grasp for power was singular. He saw himself as the only one worthy of worship.

Herod was outwitted. Matthew makes it clear that the Magi were on to Herod's schemes and took their own stance to maneuver around him. In verse 16, he reports, "When Herod realized that he had been outwitted by the Magi, he was furious." To be outwitted is to be "played with," "mocked," even made a fool. No one likes to be found as the dupe. But for an unstable, even paranoid person, such a situation would be especially challenging. Herod's response? He became furious. The word means enraged, irate. We picture a narcissistic maniac, deranged and unhinged, don't we?

Herod reacted in evil. "He gave orders to kill all the boys in Bethlehem and its vicinity who were two years old and under, in accordance with the time he had learned from the Magi" (v. 16). Such an extreme action is in keeping with his prior murderous acts when he felt threatened by his wife and sons. Considering the size of Bethlehem and the age range included in Herod's order, likely his reaction would have brought about the deaths of at least twenty boys.[4]

Herod died but his evil influence continued. Matthew's account of Herod ends in verses 19–20 with these words, "After Herod died, an angel of the Lord appeared in a dream to Joseph in Egypt and said, 'Get up, take the child and his mother and go to the land of Israel, for those who were trying to take the child's life are dead.'"

But were they? Herod's evil schemes didn't end with his life. Matthew goes on, "But when [Joseph] heard that Archelaus was reigning in Judea in place of his father Herod, he was afraid to go there" (v. 22). Instead, receiving another directive dream, Joseph took Mary and Jesus to Nazareth in Galilee (vv. 22–23).

Herod had many opportunities to recognize and relate to Jesus. Instead, Herod rejected Christmas altogether. In the end, he was "more interested in saving his throne than in saving his soul."[5]

How Did Christmas Change Herod?

Christmas changed Herod from a man who might discover faith and find freedom to one who rejected Christmas and its lessons and followed after fear. Because Herod rejected Christmas, he refused the change Christmas offers to us all. His shrewd dealings with authority led him to clench his fists around a power he didn't want to risk losing—to anyone, for any reason. A lifetime of destroying others in order to protect his own value left Herod unable to bend his being to the authority of another. With the prophesied birth of the true "King of the Jews," even if in the tiny body of a child, Herod went from paranoid worry to full-out rebellion.

In contrast to the Magi who were seekers after the ultimate Truth and the ultimate Light and who discovered and worshiped the Source of both, Herod pivoted from the pretense of turning toward the long-awaited Messiah to running from Him in rebellion. His selfish seeking led him to sinful and murderous choices. Unteachable, Herod remained untouched by the relationship God would die to create even with him. Because Herod turned away from God's love and provision and refused to learn, he rejected the only hope for true significance that is ever really available to any of us.

Christmas Can Change Us When We Learn, unlike Herod

Christmas offers us an opportunity for transformation. But how do we respond to this offer? Do we resist God's invitation to change us, or are we open to embracing our own need to learn?

So many of life's lessons boil down to how we view power. We clamor to be right, to be in control, to be recognized and valued and to fit in. Jesus's expression of power took the form of relinquishment rather than reign.

Ron Rolheiser makes the point by asking us to imagine four people in a room: a powerful dictator who rules a nation, a gifted athlete at his peak, a rock star who can captivate an audience, and a newborn baby. "Which of these is ultimately the most powerful? The irony is that the baby ultimately wields the greatest power. . . . [A little baby] can touch hearts in a way that a dictator, an athlete, or a rock star cannot. Its innocent, wordless presence, without physical strength, can transform a room and a heart in a way that guns, muscle and charisma cannot."[6]

Along these lines, the apostle Paul writes of Jesus's submitted power in Philippians 2:5–8, "Have the same mindset as Christ Jesus: Who, being in very nature God, did not consider equality with God something to be used to his own advantage; rather, he made himself nothing by taking the very nature of a servant, being made in human likeness. And being found in appearance as man, he humbled himself by becoming obedient to death—even death on a cross!"

As I look back at my own mistakes, I have to admit that some resulted from a misplaced passion for power. The wrong kind of power. Assumptions that I'm in charge. That I get to choose. That because I've always done something one way, I should continue to do it. The power promised by control and self-management rather than the humble power of a life sacrificed for others.

One of the great recent heroes of our faith was Dr. Vernon Grounds who served as the president of Denver Seminary for decades and also on the board of Our Daily Bread Ministries. For years, Dr. Grounds would pen a Christmas letter containing his learnings from the past year and send it to friends far and wide. In one issue dated Christmas, 1955, he shared what he labeled a "blessing" from a poem by Christina Rossetti:

> God harden me against myself,
> This coward with pathetic voice
> Who craves for ease and rest and joys
> Myself, arch-traitor to myself;
> My hollowest friend, my deadliest foe,
> My clog whatever road I go.
> Yet One there is can curb myself,
> Can roll the strangling load from me,
> Break off the yoke and set me free.[7]

Herod rejected the advent of Christmas and rebelled against the change Christmas offers us all. Oh, may we learn from his errors!

I'm not sure who will host Christmas this year or who will actually gather. What I do know is that I will be giving my gifts with a deep gratitude for the relationships forged over the years and with an openness to how I need to continue to grow in all my relationships. Always. From my generation to the next and then to the next and the next. I'm learning . . .

✳ ✳ ✳

Change Point: *Is there a place you are resistant to learning? Where could you be holding on to "your" power and rights and preferences and privileges rather than taking the stance of student? How might you miss God's advent in your heart by refusing His leading and His ways?*

Our Stories

How would you write your Christmas story?

CHAPTER TEN

Welcome

We hauled the many boxes containing our Christmas decorations up the stairs from the basement while our seven-year-old grandson Marcus dragged a trash bag containing Christmas stuffed animals behind him. Our day-after-Thanksgiving tradition includes putting up our tree and decorating the house inside and out. Usually, the inside falls to me and the outside to Evan and a grandson or two.

It was a warm day in Denver that year. While I arranged a nativity set in our living room, I watched my husband and grandson outside through the window. They untangled the strings of red and white lights, stretching them across and then anchoring them in place to border our flowerbed. They staked down Mr. Snowman, Mama Snowman, and Little Snowdude, representing Evan, me, and Marcus. At the front door, I fixed some evergreen boughs with twinkly lights, hung a wreath on the door, and placed a special Christmas welcome mat by the threshold. The musical accessory that timed our outdoor lights to Christmas carols was placed just so. In our final presentation moment, all the extension cords were plugged in and—*boom!*— Christmas came alive.

Up and down our street, around the corner in the apartments, and at the day-care center at the entrance to our neighborhood, similar efforts were underway. Blow-up Santas and penguins (yes—penguins!).

Reindeer and sleighs. Homemade wooden nativities with Mary and Joseph and an empty space for Jesus. Color schemes of blue and white and red and green and multi-colored bulbs.

Why do we decorate the outside of our homes for Christmas? To celebrate for sure. To break the monotony of winter months with light and fun. To engage the young ones in our families and satisfy our own desire for childlike joy. Of course!

But when Christmas became Christmas for me, I discovered another passion within my festiveness that has increased through the years. I want to grow in my love for all things "Jesus." And I want others around me to discover the difference His love makes. Decking the halls has become more than merely a tradition to carry forward. I want to *welcome* Christmas through what my home looks like on the outside and the inside, as it represents the commitment of my life on the outside and inside.

Welcome, Jesus! Come . . . change everything!

In Mark 9, Jesus uses the word *welcome* to express how we can relate to Him. Speaking of the value of children in a day when their importance was minimized until they were able to contribute to families and society, Jesus said, "Whoever welcomes one of these little children in my name welcomes me; and whoever welcomes me does not welcome me but the one who sent me" (v. 37). Jesus surprises the disciples—and all who were listening—by emphasizing that we welcome Him when we welcome the children—the vulnerable and the needy in our world—into our lives.

The word used here actually means to receive, to accept, as one would a person who is a guest.[1]

Christmas changes everything for you and me when we welcome the life-changing gift of Christmas: Jesus.

As we've followed the characters in the Christmas story together, we've seen the metamorphosis of how Christmas changes everything in each one—and because it changed them, it can change us as well. Is there one character's transformation that best matches the season of your life this year? How could you welcome that character's discovery in order to receive for yourself the change Christmas brought them?

Christmas changed Mary from a virgin to the mother of our Savior who accepted God's invitation for her life. When we accept Christmas as Mary did, we say yes to God's call on our lives and we become part of His world-changing work. Might you welcome God's gift to you in the acceptance of His calling?

Christmas changed Joseph from a grieving fiancé to a committed husband and the stepfather of Jesus. When we yield to God's design for our lives, disastrous situations can be used to bring hope and healing to us and through us to others. Could you welcome God's invitation to yield to His shaping in and through you?

Christmas changed Zechariah from a man who doubted to a father who believed in God's faithfulness. When we believe, we recognize God's work in and around us. Is there a place you have dug deeply into doubt and unbelief and yet you sense God wooing you to welcome the truth of who He is and to risk believing again?

Christmas changed Elizabeth from a disgraced, childless woman who wondered about her worth to a rejoicing mother who saw God's favor fulfilled in her life. When we rejoice in God's work in us, we can allow our joy to spill out and onto others. Is this a season when welcoming however God is working in your life could move you to rejoice in His faithfulness?

Christmas changed the shepherds from lowly workers watching over lambs to men called to worship the Lamb of God and share the good news of His arrival. When we recognize God's reality, we'll want to tell others about Him. Is God asking you to welcome the gift of sharing your faith with others so that they can come to know Him as well?

Christmas changed Simeon from a waiting man to a fulfilled follower. When we commit ourselves to waiting well, God will open our eyes to His provision. Is God asking you to welcome the opportunity to wait on Him as He brings about the eventual fulfillment of your desires?

Christmas changed Anna from a woman who worshiped in fervent hope to one who worshiped with experienced conviction. When we are faithful to worship God in the daily and the dramatic, our relationship with Him deepens. Is God asking you to welcome the routine of worship so that you can be in the right place at the right time to receive the blessing of extraordinary moments with Him?

Christmas changed the Magi from those seeking truth to those who discovered its Source. When we seek truth with sincere hearts, we will not only find it but also the One who is the truth. How is God inviting you to seek truth and its Source?

Herod rejected Christmas and so refused the change it could have brought him. When we reject God's advent, we refuse God's offer of transformation, growth, and redemption. How might you welcome learning by letting go of power and control?

Accept. Yield. Believe. Rejoice. Share. Wait. Worship. Seek. Learn. Christmas changed everything for every character who welcomed the very first story of Advent. As we tune into their journeys, we discover wisdom for our own.

Let's decorate our beings with lights and colors and boughs and bows. Let's roll out the red-carpet welcome. Let's invite our own hearts and the hearts of all we love across the welcome mat into a relationship with the Giver of all gifts who gives us the *best* gift: Jesus. The gift that changes everything.

✳ ✳ ✳

Change Point: *As you consider each character in the Christmas story and how they welcomed (or didn't welcome) Christmas, how is God nudging you to welcome Christmas this year?*

To welcome the gift of Christmas, a relationship with Jesus, simply pray this prayer or something like it:

*Dear God. I want to know you. I admit that I can't
make my life work on my own. I mess it up and make
choices that lead me away from you. Please forgive me. I want
to receive you as my Savior, and I want to follow you as my
Lord every day because I trust that you know what is best for
me. I choose to accept, yield, believe, rejoice, share, wait,
worship, seek, learn . . . and welcome. In Jesus's name, amen.*

Christmas Isn't Over

Is your tree still up? Your lights still twinkling? Are the carols repetitively looping?

There comes a time when we box Christmas up and drag it to the basement or hoist it up the attic stairs or shove it away into the storeroom. Out of sight. There to sit in the dark until the next Advent season arrives.

But Christmas isn't over when we put it back in the box. It won't be over next month, and it won't be over in July. Christmas continues as long as we allow Christmas to change us and, through us, to change our world.

The very first Christmas changed everything. And because Christmas isn't over, it can continue to change everything when we welcome the gift of Jesus in our lives. When we

Accept, like Mary.
Yield, like Joseph.
Believe, like Zechariah.
Rejoice, like Elizabeth.
Share, like the shepherds.
Wait, like Simeon.
Worship, like Anna.
Seek, like the Magi.
Learn, unlike Herod.

Let us then watch for—and welcome—the continuing Christmas. Emmanuel. God is *with* us. Today, tomorrow. Next month. Always.

Because Christmas isn't over. Christmas never ends.

NOTES

Chapter One: Accept

1. *NLT Study Bible* (Carol Stream: Tyndale House Publishers, 2008), study note, p. 1708.

2. D. A. Carson, *The NIV Zondervan Study Bible* (Grand Rapids: Zondervan, 2015), 1927–28.

3. Ruth A. Tucker, *The Biographical Bible* (Grand Rapids: Baker Books, 2013), 285.

4. Johannes P. Louw and Eugene A. Nida, *Greek-English Lexicon of the New Testament: Based on Semantic Domains, vol. 1*, electronic ed. of the 2nd ed. (New York: United Bible Societies, 1996), 314.

5. Bill Crowder, *Windows on Christmas* (Grand Rapids: Our Daily Bread Publishing, 2021), 38.

6. Lynn Cohick, *Women in the World of the Earliest Christians* (Grand Rapids: Baker Academic, 2009), 38.

7. John A. Martin, "Luke," in John F. Walvoord and Roy B. Zuck, eds., *The Bible Knowledge Commentary: New Testament* (Wheaton, IL: David C Cook, 1983), 205.

8. Johannes P. Louw and Eugene A. Nida, *Greek-English Lexicon of the New Testament: Based on Semantic Domains, vol. 1*, electronic ed. of the 2nd ed. (New York: United Bible Societies, 1996), 741.

9. R. L. Thomas, *New American Standard Hebrew-Aramaic and Greek Dictionaries: Updated Edition* (Anaheim, CA: Foundation Publications, 1998).

10. Jean Fleming, "The Practice of Pondering," *Monica Sharman Editing* (blog), June 20, 2014, https://monicasharman.wordpress.com/2014/06/20/the-practice-of-pondering-by-jean-fleming/.

Chapter Two: Yield

1. D. A. Carson, *The NIV Zondervan Study Bible* (Grand Rapids: Zondervan, 2015), study note for Matthew 1:18–19, 1927.

2. Paul D. Gardner, ed., *New International Encyclopedia of Bible Characters* (Grand Rapids: Zondervan, 1995), 370.

3. Leon Morris, *The Gospel according to Matthew, The Pillar New Testament Commentary*, ed. D. A. Carson (Grand Rapids: Eerdmans, 1992), 32.

4. Elisa Morgan, *The Beauty of Broken* (Nashville: Thomas Nelson, 2013).

Chapter Three: Believe

1. Paul D. Gardner, ed., *New International Encyclopedia of Bible Characters* (Grand Rapids: Zondervan, 1995), 674

2. D. A. Carson, *The NIV Zondervan Study Bible* (Grand Rapids: Zondervan, 2015), study note for Luke 1:9, 2067.

3. H. D. M. Spence-Jones, ed., *St. Luke*, The Pulpit Commentary, vol. 1, ed. Joseph S. Exell (London/New York: Funk & Wagnalls, 1909), 4.

4. John A. Martin, "Luke," in John F. Walvoord and Roy B. Zuck, eds., *The Bible Knowledge Commentary: New Testament* (Wheaton, IL: David C Cook, 1983), 203.

5. Robert H. Stein, *Luke*, The New American Commentary, vol. 24 (Nashville: Broadman & Holman, 1992), 77.

6. Spence-Jones, *St. Luke*, 5.

7. Trent C. Butler, *Luke*, Holman New Testament Commentary, vol. 3, ed. Max Anders (Nashville: B&H Publishing, 2000), 9.

Chapter Four: Rejoice

1. Paul D. Gardner, ed., *New International Encyclopedia of Bible Characters* (Grand Rapids: Zondervan, 1995), 159.

2. Edith Deen, *All of the Women of the Bible* (New York: HarperCollins, 1983), 171. Original "Elisabeth" updated to "Elizabeth."

Chapter Five: Share

1. Bill Crowder, *Windows on Christmas* (Grand Rapids: Our Daily Bread Publishing, 2007), 48.

2. H. D. M. Spence-Jones, ed., *St. Luke*, The Pulpit Commentary, vol. 1, ed. Joseph S. Exell (London/New York: Funk & Wagnalls, 1909), 38.

3. D. A. Carson, *The NIV Zondervan Study Bible* (Grand Rapids: Zondervan, 2015), Luke 2:14, 2071.

4. Johannes P. Louw and Eugene A. Nida, *Greek-English Lexicon of the New Testament: Based on Semantic Domains, vol. 1,* electronic ed. of the 2nd ed. (New York: United Bible Societies, 1996), 315.

5. Louw and Nida, *Greek-English Lexicon*, 328.

Chapter Six: Wait

1. D. A. Carson, *The NIV Zondervan Study Bible* (Grand Rapids: Zondervan, 2015), study note for Luke 2:25, 2070.

2. "Simeon Meaning," Abarim Publications, accessed January 9, 2022, https://www.abarim-publications.com/Meaning/Simeon.html.

3. Johannes P. Louw and Eugene A. Nida, *Greek-English Lexicon of the New Testament: Based on Semantic Domains, vol. 1,* electronic ed. of the 2nd ed. (New York: United Bible Societies, 1996), 311.

4. Dr. Mark Young, "Merry Christmas Denver Seminary Alumni," December 13, 2020, https://vimeo.com/490576514.

Chapter Seven: Worship

1. Paul D. Gardner, ed., *New International Encyclopedia of Bible Characters* (Grand Rapids: Zondervan, 1995), 823.

2. *NLT Study Bible* (Carol Stream: Tyndale House Publishers, 2008), study note from Luke 2:36–37, 1705.

3. *NLT Study Bible*, study note from Luke 2:36–38, 1705.

4. H. D. M. Spence-Jones, ed., *St. Luke*, The Pulpit Commentary, vol. 1, ed. Joseph S. Exell (London/New York: Funk & Wagnalls, 1909), 41.

5. Trent C. Butler, *Luke*, Holman New Testament Commentary, vol. 3, ed. Max Anders (Nashville: B&H Publishing, 2000), 33.

6. Bill Crowder, *Windows on Christmas* (Grand Rapids: Our Daily Bread Publishing, 2007, 2021), 109.

7. Edith Deen, *All of the Women of the Bible* (New York: HarperCollins, 1983), 175.

8. Brother Lawrence with Harold Myra, *The Practice of the Presence of God: Experience the Spiritual Classic through 40 Days of Devotion* (Grand Rapids: Discovery House, 2017).

Chapter Eight: Seek

1. Paul D. Gardner, ed., *New International Encyclopedia of Bible Characters* (Grand Rapids: Zondervan, 1995), 431.

2. Walter Bauer, *A Greek-English Lexicon of the New Testament and Other Early Christian Literature*, 2nd ed., trans. William F. Arndt and F. Wilbur Gingrich (Chicago: University of Chicago Press, 1979).

3. Ruth A. Tucker, *The Biographical Bible* (Grand Rapids: Baker Books, 2013), 288.

4. Leon Morris, *The Gospel according to Matthew*, The Pillar New Testament Commentary, ed. D. A. Carson (Grand Rapids: Eerdmans, 1992), 36.

5. Louis A. Barbieri Jr., "Matthew," in John F. Walvoord and Roy B. Zuck, eds., *The Bible Knowledge Commentary: New Testament* (Wheaton: David C Cook, 1983), 21.

6. Johannes P. Louw and Eugene A. Nida, *Greek-English Lexicon of the New Testament: Based on Semantic Domains, vol. 2,* electronic ed. of the 2nd ed. (New York: United Bible Societies, 1996), 539.

7. Morris, *Gospel according to Matthew*, 41.

8. Barbieri, "*Matthew*," 22.

9. Jamie Carter, "How, When and Where You Can See 'Christmas Star' Planets Then Shooting Stars on the Solstice This Week," *Forbes*, December 18, 2020, https://www.forbes.com/sites/jamiecartereurope/2020/12/18/how-when-and-where-you-can-see-christmas-star-planets-then-shooting-stars-on-the-solstice-this-week/?sh=1f5740ea5348.

10. Morris, *Gospel according to Matthew*, 41.

Chapter Nine: Learn

1. *NLT Study Bible* (Carol Stream: Tyndale House Publishers, 2008), study note for Matthew 2:3, 1578.

2. *NLT Study Bible*, study note for Matthew 2:3, 1578.

3. J. D. Douglas and Merrill C. Tenney, *Zondervan Illustrated Bible Dictionary* (Grand Rapids: Zondervan, 2011), 602.

4. Stuart K. Weber, *Matthew*, Holman New Testament Commentary, vol. 1, ed. Max Anders (Nashville: Broadman & Holman Publishers, 2000), 21.

5. Leon Morris, *The Gospel according to Matthew, The Pillar New Testament Commentary*, ed. D. A. Carson (Grand Rapids: Eerdmans, 1992), 37.

6. Ron Rolheiser, "The Power of Powerlessness," RonRolheiser.com, May 6, 2012, https://ronrolheiser.com/the-power-of-powerlessness/#.YbOU3X3ML0p.

7. Christina Rossetti, "Who Shall Deliver Me?" https://victorianweb.org/authors/crossetti/delucia7.html.

Chapter Ten: Welcome

1. Johannes P. Louw and Eugene A. Nida, *Greek-English Lexicon of the New Testament: Based on Semantic Domains, vol. 2*, electronic ed. of the 2nd ed. (New York: United Bible Societies, 1996), 452.

Spread the Word
by Doing One Thing.

- Give a copy of this book as a gift.
- Share the QR code link via your social media.
- Write a review of this book on your blog, favorite bookseller's website, or at ODB.org/store.
- Recommend this book to your church, small group, or book club.

Connect with us. 🅕 🅞 🐦

Our Daily Bread Publishing
PO Box 3566, Grand Rapids, MI 49501, USA
Email: books@odb.org